THE CREATIVE CHRISTMAS BOOK

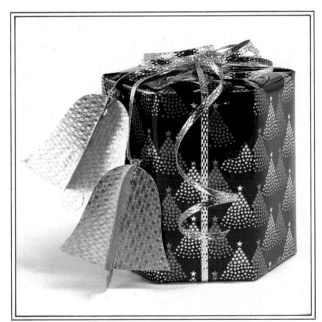

THE CREATIVE CHRISTMAS BOOK

Longmeadow Press

This 1989 edition published by
Longmeadow Press,
201 High Ridge Road,
Stamford, CT 06904.

©Salamander Books Ltd. 1988

ISBN 0-681-40767-0

CREDITS

Contributors: Rosalind Burdett, Jan Hall, Karen Lansdown, Suzie Major,
Susy Smith and Sarah Waterkeyn

Editor: Jilly Glassborow

Designers: Kathy Gummer and Barry Savage

Photographers: Terry Dilliway and Steve Tanner

Typeset by: The Old Mill, London

Color separation by: Fotographics Ltd, London — Hong Kong

Printed in Italy

CONTENTS

INTRODUCTION

Christmas Decorations   6

Festive Table Decorations   34

Festive Floral Designs   52

Gift Wrapping   70

Index   96

It's that time of year again when our thoughts turn to parties and presents, when we bedeck our homes with paper chains, tinsel and holly, and wear funny hats at table. And what better way to get into the spirit of Christmas than to make your own decorations — hours of fun for all the family and so much cheaper than buying them.

With fully illustrated step-by-step instructions this colourful book will show you how to make over 150 dazzling designs. There are Christmas tree decorations, paper chains, stars, bells, baubles, garlands, greeting card trellises, and party hats and masks. And for that special festive dinner party or the big day itself there's a stunning range of designs to brighten up your table — centrepieces, napkin folds, placemats, name cards, crackers and other attractive table gifts.

Flowers are always a favourite at Christmas and, as well as featuring some colourful fresh flower displays, there's an exciting array of dried flower designs that will see you through the whole festive season — and on to the next! The book ends with a section on gift wrapping that's packed with original ideas for making your own paper, tags and decorative ties and bows. There are also lots of ingenious ways to disguise gifts such as records and bottles to keep the recipient guessing.

Of all the Christmas decorations, the Christmas tree is without doubt the most dazzling. This chapter contains a wealth of designs for decorating trees, including fake baubles, mini crackers, edible stars, sugar bells, paper lanterns and many more. Or, if you prefer a more sophisticated look, you could copy one of the stunning, though slightly more expensive, designs shown on the opening pages. The chapter also features colourful ribbon trees — a good substitute for the real thing — a host of pretty paper chains and garlands, some ingenious ways of displaying Christmas cards, lots of delightful wall hangings and a small but fun range of party hats and masks.

GO FOR GOLD

This traditional tree (right) is covered in tinsel, baubles and lametta (icicles), all in gold. A similarly elegant effect could be achieved using silver on a fake white tree; or if you have a fake silver tree, try bright pink or blue. Stick to one colour only for the most professional-looking results. If the children want to hang chocolate figures on the tree, buy some colour-coordinated ones!

Start by hanging a string of white or gold lights over the tree. Lights always make the vital difference to a Christmas tree; it is lovely to switch them on when night falls. Next, trail thick gold tinsel around the branches, concealing the light cord.

The baubles can then go on, followed by strands of lametta (icicles). At the top of the tree you could place an angel or star. The star shape shown is made from loops of tinsel — simple, but very effective. The finishing touch is a pile of gold-wrapped presents at the foot of the tree. Choose some shiny wrapping paper and cover empty boxes. If you put your presents under the tree, add a few fakes too; otherwise it looks terribly bare once the presents have been opened.

LOVELY LACE

TARTAN TIES

For a more old-fashioned look, omit sparkly baubles and lights, and stick to lace, ribbons and a few paper doilies. Start with some silk flowers wired onto the branches or simply placed on them. Take some wide lace edging and thread thin rose-coloured ribbon through the straight edge; gather it into a rosette over the ends of the branches. Allow the ends to hang down as shown.

In the gaps place some fans made from circular white paper doilies, cut in half and lightly pleated. Onto these, staple little ribbon bows, again letting the ends hang down. The pot the tree is standing in has been wrapped in plain brown paper and decorated with a large paper fan made from a rectangular doily.

Here is an unusual and very attractive way of decorating the tree. First take a set of candle lights and fasten them onto the tree. Next, you need a large bunch of gypsophilia (baby's breath). You should be able to get this even at Christmas from a good florist.

Split up the gypsophilia and simply poke it into the tree until all the gaps between branches are filled. Although bought fresh, gypsophilia should last a few days on the tree. Next you need a piece of tartan fabric, about half a metre (yard). Cut it into strips and tie them into bows on the ends of the branches. Cover the pot or stand in coloured crepe paper and tie a large bow around it.

This is especially for the kids; but be warned: you will have to exert extreme control, or the tree will be looking very bare by Boxing Day (December 26th)! On this tree we have hung iced cookies (see the instructions on page 12), little meringues and, for the grown-ups, some Amaretti biscuits — nice with the after-dinner port!

Also hung on the tree are some cute wooden cut-outs in the shape of Santa Claus, teddy bears and other favourites. You could easily make them into a mobile after Christmas, to hang in a child's bedroom. To complete the effect, some huge gingerbread men, one at the top of the tree, some in the lower branches — perhaps too well within reach of small fingers!

This is a very pretty way to treat a synthetic white tree. The lights used are large, cone-shaped white tree lights. Next, hang on lots of baubles: pastel satin, white satin with pink bows, silver with embroidered flowers.

Now simply take lengths of pastel ribbon, such as the pink, green and blue shown here, and tie them onto the ends of the branches — some in bows, the others hanging down in strands. Tie a large bow at the top of the tree. Cover the pot or stand in silver wrapping paper, and tie a large pastel bow around it.

SUGAR BELLS

These ornaments are very easy to make; all you need are some bells from last year's tree. If you haven't got any, look for suitable moulds in the cake decorating section of a department store. Take some ordinary granulated sugar, put a few spoonfuls in a dish, and moisten it with food colouring.

When the colouring is thoroughly mixed in, push the sugar into a bell mould, pressing it in firmly to fill the entire cavity.

Now simply tap the sugar bell out of the mould. Leave the bells to dry out overnight. To hang them on the tree, cut out a little tissue paper flower, thread a loop through it and glue it to the top of the bell. (These ornaments are not edible, and should be placed out of the reach of small children.)

PING PONG PUDDINGS

Here is another cute tree decoration that is fun to make: tiny Christmas puddings. You start with ordinary ping pong balls. Spear each one onto a fine knitting needle and paint it brown. After two or three coats, for a dark rich colour, finish off with a clear varnish to give the 'puddings' a lovely shine.

Now take some modelling clay, the sort you can bake in the oven, and roll it into a ball, the same size as the ping pong balls. Over this, mould a thick circle of white clay, to look like custard sauce. Bake this in the oven, and then remove it from the clay ball straight away, and pop it onto a pudding, so that it fits as it cools down and hardens. Don't forget to poke a hole in the top at this point.

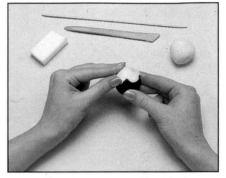

When the clay is cold, glue it to the pudding. Now take a double thread, knot the end and thread it through the pudding from the bottom upwards. Trim off the ends, then finish each pudding by gluing on foil holly leaves and red bead berries.

HANGING BOXES

These little boxes make charming tree decorations. If you haven't got any suitable ones that you can wrap for the tree, you can easily make your own from cardboard. For a cube, you need to mark out a Latin cross shape. The lower arm of the cross should be twice as long as the top and side arms. Also add a 1.5cm (½ in) border to all arms except the top one for gluing the cube together.

Fold along all the lines as shown, then bring the cube together, gluing all the sides in place.

Now simply wrap the box in attractive paper, and tie it with ribbons and bows to look like a parcel. Pop it on or under the tree.

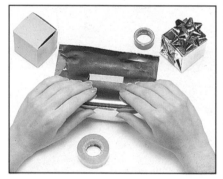

SATIN 'PRESENTS'

These pretty ornaments can be made any size. For a cube shape the pattern is a Latin cross (as shown), the long piece being twice the length of the others; all the other sides must be of equal length. Cut this shape out in satin, then cut a piece of iron-on interfacing, 1cm (½in) smaller all round. Iron on the interfacing. Also iron in creases to form the sides of the cube.

Placing right sides together, sew all the seams, using a small running stitch, cutting into the corners and using the interfacing edge as a seamline.

Leave one edge open so that you can turn the cube right side out. Stuff it with polyester filling, then slipstitch the opening edges together. Decorate the cube with ribbon and bows, then set it on a branch of your Christmas tree. For a rectangular box, simply widen the long section of the cross. The round box is a purchased box with satin glued onto it.

Another fun tree decoration that will last from year to year. Make a tree-shaped and a pot-shaped pattern out of cardboard. Now cut the shapes out in two different colours of felt, cutting two each of tree and pot. Place the two tree shapes together, and work buttonhole stitch around the edges, leaving the trunk end open.

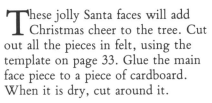

These jolly Santa faces will add Christmas cheer to the tree. Cut out all the pieces in felt, using the template on page 33. Glue the main face piece to a piece of cardboard. When it is dry, cut around it.

Stuff the tree lightly with a little filling. Now buttonhole stitch around the pot, leaving the top open. Slip the trunk into the pot, and then lightly stuff the pot. Sew the tree and pot together at the sides.

Sew a little bow to the top of the pot, and decorate the tree with sequins and tinsel. Fix some gold or silver thread under the star on the top of the tree, so you can hang it up.

All you have to do now is glue on all the other pieces. The nose and cheeks are affixed before the moustache, which goes on top.

Place a loop of thread under the circle on the top of the hat, to hang up the face. Glue on two dark sequins to represent the eyes.

These decorations are made from a basic recipe of 250g (8oz, 2 cups) plain (all-purpose) flour, 125g (4oz, 2 tablespoons) butter, 150g (5oz, 5/8 cup) caster (fine granulated) sugar and 2 egg yolks. Cream butter and sugar until fluffy, add egg yolks and flour, and mix them into a firm dough. Roll the pasty out until it is about 1cm (½ in) thick, and cut out the chosen shapes.

Skewer a hole in each, so that you can push a thread through later. (This may close up during baking — in which case you will have to pierce another hole in them when they are cold — but very carefully, as the biscuits have a habit of breaking!) Put them onto a greased baking sheet, and bake them at 180°C (350°F), or gas mark 4, for 15 minutes.

When the cookies are cool, make up some fairly stiff icing using icing (confectioner's) sugar and water, and ice them. Thread them onto some waxed thread — or ribbon if the hole is big enough — and hang them on the tree straight away; they won't stay there very long!

Make a pattern for a Christmas stocking and cut it out double in one piece by placing the pattern on the fold of a double layer of felt. Cut a strip of fake fur to fit the stocking, about 5cm (2in) deep. Catch the fur to the felt, top and bottom, by hand, with small stitches.

Now overcast the two sides of the stocking together, starting at the ankle and working around the foot and up the front. Turn the stocking right side out.

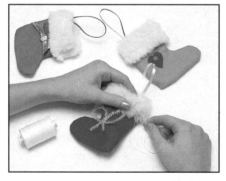

Turn the fur down about 2.5cm (1in) to the right side, catching it down around the edge. Decorate the stocking with sequins, bows, etc., and sew a loop of ribbon just inside the edge to hang it from the tree.

By the time Christmas arrives, you may not have much extra cash for Christmas tree baubles, so these colourful fakes are a great way of economizing. First cut some circles, with a little loop on the top, from some lightweight cardboard. Now mark out a pattern on each in pencil. Simple zigzags and curved lines are effective, but not too complicated to fill in.

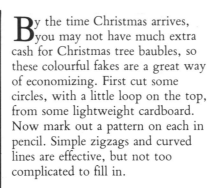

Paint each bauble with several different colours, waiting for each to dry before painting the next. If you have some gold or silver paint, make good use of this, as it is very effective. Use black to make definite lines between colours.

These miniature crackers can be hung on the Christmas tree or on the wall. First take a piece of cartridge (drawing) paper or light cardboard about 8cm (3in) wide and long enough to roll into a tube. Hold it together with a little sticky tape.

When the baubles are dry, attach some thread, ribbon or, as shown, some tinsel wire, so that you can hang them up.

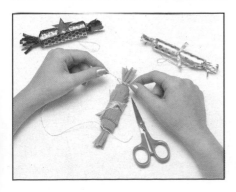

Cut a piece of crepe paper or foil twice as long as the tube, and roll the tube in it. Stick the edges together with double-sided tape. Squeeze the paper together at both ends, and tie some thread around them. Fluff out the ends and make small cuts in them to make a fringe.

To decorate the cracker, cut some extra, narrow pieces of crepe paper or foil, fringe them at the edges and wrap them around the tube as before. Alternatively, tie a bow round the cracker or stick a silver star in the middle. Tie a length of ribbon or sparkly twine to the ends by which to hang the cracker.

If you haven't any shiny bells for the Christmas tree, it's not difficult to make some from foil, beads and a little string. First take a saucer and mark around it onto the back of some coloured foil. Cut out the circle, then fold it in half, and cut along the fold line. Fold each half of the circle into a cone and glue it in place.

For the clapper, string a bead onto a length of thread — preferably waxed — and tie a knot over the bead. Lay the thread against the bell so that the clapper is at the right level, then tie a knot level with the hole in the top. This prevents the string from being pulled through the hole when threaded. Pull the string through the hole from the inside and thread on a smaller bead at the top; knot in place.

Finish each bell by dabbing a little glue around the bottom edge and sprinkling on some glitter. When you have made three bells, string them together, and attach them to a ring so that they can be hung on the tree. Wind a little tinsel wire around the string, and tie a couple of bows for that final touch of glamour.

These miniature lanterns make attractive Christmas tree ornaments. First take a piece of foil-covered paper 11cm (5½in) square. Fold it in half, and rule a line 1.5cm (¾in) from the loose edges. Now rule lines 1cm (½in) apart, from the fold up to this first line. Cut along these lines and open out the sheet of paper.

Hold the paper with the cuts running vertically, and glue the two sides together. When this is firm, set the lantern on the table and gently push the top down to make the sides poke outwards.

Finally, cut a strip of matching paper 13cm (5in) long and 1cm (½in) wide. Dab some glue on each end, and glue the strip onto the inside of the lantern, at the top, for a handle.

|

A shiny foil star makes a striking decoration for the top of the Christmas tree. Using the instructions on page 23, cut out a pattern in cardboard. Now cut two squares of cardboard, slightly larger than the star template, and cover each side with a different coloured foil. Next cut out two stars, one from each foil-covered square.

This traditional English Christmas tree-top decoration makes a charming addition to the festivities. Using a saucer, cut a circle out of silver foil paper. Cut the circle in half and fold one half into a cone, taping it in place.

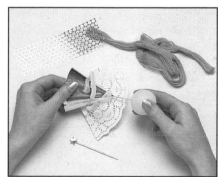

Take a ruler and pencil, and placing the ruler between two opposite points, mark a line on each star from one point to the centre. Cut along these lines and then simply slot the two stars together.

Take a pink pipe cleaner and tape it to the back of the cone; then bend it into arms and hands. On top of this fix a triangle of doily to represent wings, using double-sided tape. For the head, take an ordinary ping pong ball and skewer it onto a wooden toothpick (or cocktail stick). Push the stick into the cone.

Use sticky tape to hold the points together and attach a piece of green garden wire to one set of points. You can then use the wire to attach the star to the tree. Finish the star by dabbing some glue onto the points and sprinkling glitter over them for an extra-sparkly effect.

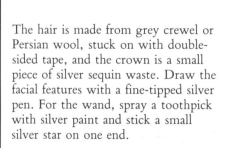

The hair is made from grey crewel or Persian wool, stuck on with double-sided tape, and the crown is a small piece of silver sequin waste. Draw the facial features with a fine-tipped silver pen. For the wand, spray a toothpick with silver paint and stick a small silver star on one end.

This unusual decoration adds a festive touch to a mirror or favourite painting. Make it in separate sections, one to be horizontal, the other vertical. You need fake ivy, fern and other foliage, plus pine cones, gold baubles and gold curling gift wrap ribbon. Cut off the long stems and wire everything up as shown, using florist's wire.

For the top section gradually lay pieces on top of one another, binding the wires and stems together with tape as you go along. The arrangement should be relatively long and narrow.

For the second section, use the same technique, but make the arrangement fuller. Hold the two pieces as you would like them to sit on the frame, and wire them together. Bend the stem wires back so that they will slip over the frame and hold the arrangement in place.

These small fir trees are fun to decorate and add a festive touch to any Christmas sideboard or buffet table. For a gold tree, make small bows of fine gold ribbon. Drape a string of gold beads in a spiral over the tree, starting at the top, then fix the bows in between the loops of beads.

Wrap some tartan ribbon around the pot and secure the ends with fabric glue. Make a separate bow and attach it with glue or pins,

If you have no room for a proper Christmas tree, this would be a good alternative — small but spectacular. First take a medium-sized plastic flower pot, about 15cm (6in) in diameter, and fill it, up to about 2.5cm (1in) from the rim, with fast-drying cement or wood filler. When this is just setting, insert a piece of 1.5cm (½in) dowelling about 40cm (16in) long.

When the filler is dry, spray paint the pot, the dowelling and the 'earth' surface gold. Lay it down to spray it, and when one side is dry, roll it over and spray the other side. The whole thing — especially the pot — will need a couple of coats.

When the paint is dry, take a ball of florists' foam at least 12cm (5in) in diameter and push it on top of the dowelling.

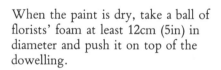

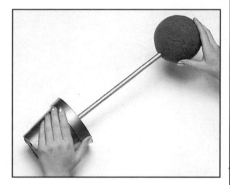

Now take short lengths of deep red and green satin ribbon, gold ribbon, shiny baubles and gold tinsel, and wire them all up, ready to push into the foam. Start with about a dozen of each; you can add to them as you go along, if necessary.

Start inserting the wires into the sphere, arranging the ribbons and baubles until it is covered, with no foam showing through. Finally wire up some curling gift wrap ribbon and insert it into the bottom of the ball. (Curl the ribbon by running the blunt edge of a pair of scissors along it.) Wind gold tinsel around the 'trunk' of the tree, and tie a large bow around the pot as a finishing touch.

Turn each tube right side out and stuff it with polyester filling, polystyrene beads or old tights (pantyhose) cut into strips. Have a stick handy to help push the stuffing down the tube. Turn in the raw edges and sew them together.

Wind narrow red ribbon around the green tube, sewing it in place at each end to secure. When you have made all three tubes, plait them together loosely and join the ends together. Cover the point where they join with a large bow made from net, and add three small net bows around the ring.

This is a very effective fabric wreath, which can be brought out for Christmas year after year. All you need are three strips of fabric, in red, green and white, about 150cm (60in) long and 18cm (7in) wide. Sew them into tubes, right side facing, leaving one end open.

Thread tinsel through the wreath, and decorate with golden baubles, tied on with thread at the back. To finish, add some curly strands of gold gift wrap ribbon. Curl the ribbon by running the blunt edge of a pair of scissors along it.

This makes an ideal Christmas wall hanging, particularly if you haven't room for a real tree. First make a paper pattern of a tree, about 75cm (30in) high and 59cm (23½in) wide at the widest point across the bottom branches. Also cut a pattern for the pot, about 25cm (10in) high. Make it about as wide as the base of the tree, with a slightly wider, 8cm (3in) deep 'rim' at the top as shown.

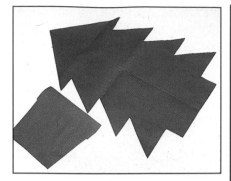

Cut out two pieces of green felt from the tree pattern and two pieces of red for the pot. Also cut out a piece of wadding (batting) for each. The wadding for the pot should be about 4.5cm (1¾in) shorter, since the rim of the pot will be turned down. On the front of the tree mark diagonal lines for the branches as shown.

Place the tree pieces together, with wadding on top. Pin, tack (baste), then stitch 1cm (³⁄₈in) from the edge, leaving the lower edge open. Clip the corners and turn tree right side out. Stitch along marked lines. Make up the pot, sewing up to 4cm (1½in) from the top. Turn it right side out and slip the tree inside; sew it in place. Sew the upper sides of the pot together and turn the rim down.

To decorate the tree cut out little pockets of red felt and sew them in place as shown. Insert little gifts — either real ones or gift-wrapped cardboard squares.

Finish off by adding plenty of ribbons and bells. Curtain rings also look good covered in ribbon and sewn on. Sew a loop to the top of the tree to hang it by.

TINSEL BELLS

All you really need for this decoration is some garden wire, a little bit of tinsel and a couple of baubles; but a pair of pliers will make it easier to manipulate the wire. Bend the wire into the shape of a bell. (You could, of course, try much more complicated shapes once you get the hang of it.)

Now just wind tinsel around the wire until it is completely covered. A couple of layers will be sufficient.

Finish off with a bauble, tied on to represent the clapper, and some bright red ribbon to tie the bells together.

GRACEFUL BELLS

This decoration can be made with tissue paper, coloured aluminium foil, thin cardboard or construction paper. Cut between six and twelve bell shapes (depending on the thickness of the paper you use). Fold each shape in half and then open it out again.

Lay the cut-outs carefully on top of each other with all the creases in the centre. Now take a needle and thread, and starting at the top, make three long stitches down the middle. Bring the needle up and over the bottom to secure the shapes in place. Next make a small stitch between each long stitch. At the top, knot the two ends together.

Ease the bell open, piece by piece, until it forms a rounded shape. You could easily do exactly the same thing with other shapes such as a heart, ball or tree.

SILVER BELLS

HOOP-LA!

To make these pretty silver bells, just cut out two bell shapes from cardboard, using the template on page 33. Peel the backing off some silver sticky-backed plastic and place the cut-outs on top, pressing firmly; then cut around them.

Glue the loops at the top of the bells together, spreading the bell shapes apart as shown.

Curl some gift wrap ribbon by running the blunt edge of a scissors blade along it; attach the ribbon to the bells. Finish off with a bow tied through the loops and some tiny birds cut from foil paper. The template for these is superimposed on the bell template.

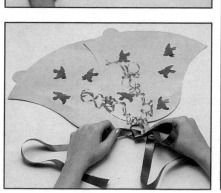

This Christmas wreath is based on a child's plastic hoop, and makes a delightful decoration for the wall or mantelpiece. First of all you need a plastic hoop; any size will do. Cut long strips of wadding (batting) and wind them around the hoop, holding the edges in place with sticky tape. We gave it two layers of medium-weight wadding.

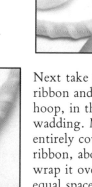

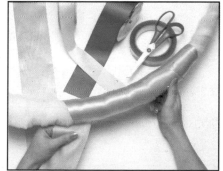

Next take some 8cm- (3in)-wide ribbon and wind it firmly around the hoop, in the opposite direction to the wadding. Make sure the wadding is entirely covered. Take a contrasting ribbon, about 6cm (2in) wide, and wrap it over the first ribbon, leaving equal spaces between the loops. Repeat with a third ribbon, 4cm (1½in) wide.

Make sure each ribbon starts and finishes in the same place so that all the joins are together. This will be the top of the hoop. Wind tinsel around the hoop, over the ribbons. Pin or staple a wide piece of ribbon over all the joins at the top. Tape a cluster of ribbon, tinsel, baubles and bells at the top and add a large bow to finish off.

EIGHT-POINTED STAR

SNOWFLAKE

A large foil star to hang in the centre of the ceiling or over the fireplace. Try it out on a piece of ordinary paper first, as it is a little fiddly. Cut a piece of foil paper about 45cm (18in) square. Fold it in half from corner to corner, then in half twice again, making a small triangle.

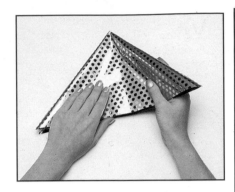

You can always have snow at Christmas, even when the sun is shining outside. Make this snowflake in foil or in plain white paper and hang it over a window-pane. First take a square of paper, fold it into quarters, then in half diagonally, then lastly back on itself as shown.

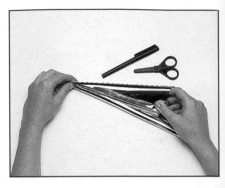

Bend the single-fold edge over to the edge with three folds. Open it out, and rule two lines from the corners at the base of the triangle to the centre crease. Cut along these two lines.

Make a pattern of the chosen design, then mark it on the folded paper with a black felt pen. Shade the areas that are to be cut away, then cut them out. Open out the snowflake. If you use a very flimsy foil, glue the snowflake onto a piece of paper, and cut out around it. This will make it easier to hang.

Refold the crease and rule two more lines, forming a small triangle as seen here. Cut this out. Now snip the point off and open the star out. Glue it to another piece of thicker foil paper for backing and cut the star out carefully when the glue has dried. Finish it off with a ribbon rosette in the centre.

Finally, decorate the snowflake with sequins in bright jewel colours. The more patience you have, the more sequins you will use and the better it will look!

Make these shiny decorations from foil wrapping paper. Cut out eight circles in each of the following diameters: 9cm (3½in), 7.5cm (3in) and 6cm (2¼in). Then from cardboard cut out four circles 2cm (¾in) in diameter and two of 1.5cm (½in) for the centres. Fold the largest foil circles into quarters and staple four of them onto a large cardboard circle.

In the same way, staple the other four foil circles to another cardboard circle. Glue the two cardboard circles together with a string between them. Leave a long piece hanging below for the other two balls. Fluff out the edges of foil to make a good shape.

This simple star can be hung on the wall or from the ceiling. First make the pattern for the star. Using a ruler and protractor, draw an equilateral triangle (each angle is 60°). Cut out the triangle and use it as a pattern to make another one. Then glue one triangle over the other to form the star. Use this pattern to cut a star from foil paper.

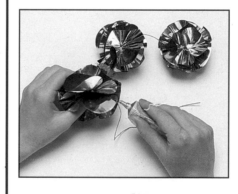

Now make the other two balls in the same way, using the smaller cardboard circles for the tiniest. Fix the balls to the string as you go.

Fold the star in half three times between opposite points. Next fold it in half three times between opposite angles as shown. Every angle and point should now have a fold in it.

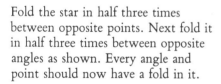

The star will now easily bend into its sculptured shape. Make a small hole in its top point with a hole punch or a skewer, then put some thread through the hole to hang it up.

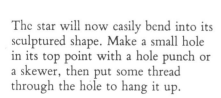

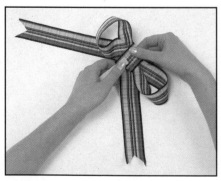
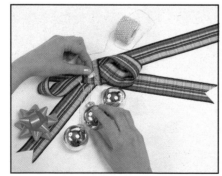
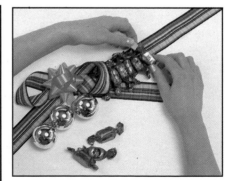

For those with a sugary tooth, here is a garland covered in brightly wrapped sweets — to be enjoyed long after the party is over. Cut a length of ribbon about 135cm (54in) long and mark the centre. Next cut three 112cm (45in) lengths of ribbon and make them up into three bows, stapling the loops into an open position as shown and trimming the ends into points.

Tape the bows onto each end and onto the centre of the main ribbon length. Then use silver thread to hang clusters of baubles from the centre of the bows. (Hang the baubles at varying lengths for the best effect.) Glue the threads to the centre of the bows and cover them up with an adhesive ribbon rosette.

Decorate some sweets with silver stars and staple them along the top edge of the ribbon between the bows. Use double-sided tape to attach the underside of the sweets to the ribbon. Finally, sew curtain rings onto the back of the ribbon for hanging the garland.

For the rosettes, cut a circle of silver cardboard, 10cm (4in) across. Take a piece of ribbon 80cm (32in) long, fold it in half and staple it to the centre of the circle. Trim the ribbon ends into points. Staple the sweets in a circle around the cardboard as shown, then stick a ribbon star in the centre. Using sticky tape, attach a curtain ring to the back of the circle for hanging up the rosette.

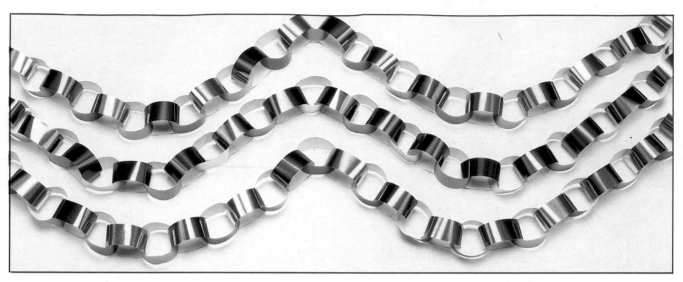

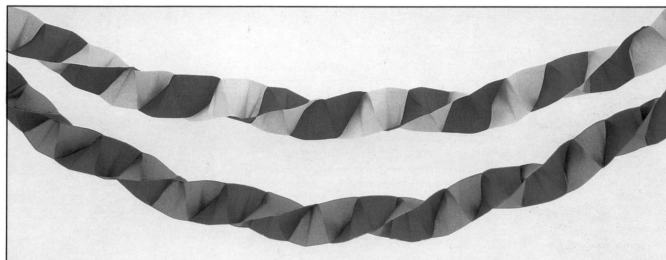

This simple paper chain takes only a few minutes to make. All you need are two different-coloured crepe papers and a touch of glue. Cut 7.5cm (3in) off the end of each crepe paper roll. Place the strips at right angles to each other, and glue one end over the other as shown.

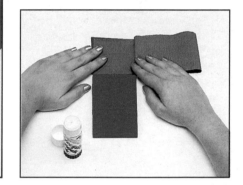

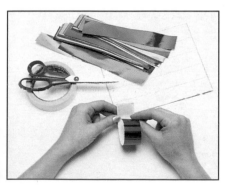

Bright-coloured foil paper makes a festive version of the simple link chain. Begin by cutting lots of strips about 18 by 3cm (7 by 1¼in). Stick the ends of the first strip together with double-sided tape (neater and quicker than glue) to make a link.

Bring the lower strip up and fold it over the other, then fold the right-hand strip over to the left as shown.

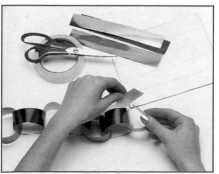

Now simply thread the next strip through and stick the ends together. Continue in this way, alternating the colours, until the chain is as long as you want it.

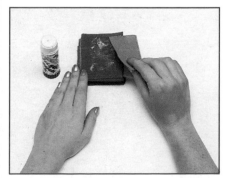

That's all there is to it; just keep folding the strips over each other alternately until you reach the end. Glue them together at the ends and trim off any extra bits.

This graceful paper chain is made from circular pieces of tissue paper. First cut two circles of cardboard and lots of circles of tissue paper, all 10cm (4in) in diameter. Take about ten tissue paper circles and fold them together in four. If you use more than about ten layers, the folds won't be as good.

Now make two curved cuts as shown, from the single-folded edge almost to the double folds. Open out the circles. Glue the centre of the first circle to the middle of one cardboard circle.

Next, take the second tissue circle and glue it to the first at the top and bottom. Glue the third circle to the centre of the second circle. Continue in this way, remembering to glue alternate circles in the same place at the top and bottom. If you alter the positioning you will spoil the effect. Finally glue the other cardboard circle to the last tissue circle to complete the garland.

Another simple garland made from tissue paper. Cut out a cardboard pattern from the template on page 33. Now cut out lots of flower shapes from tissue paper, using several different colours.

To start the garland, dab a little glue (one that won't soak through the thin paper) onto alternate petals of the first flower. Place the second flower on top and press them together.

Now on the second flower dab glue on the petals lying between those glued on the first flower. Take the third flower and press it firmly on top. Continue in this way, gluing petals in alternate positions, until the garland is long enough. Cut two extra cardboard shapes from the pattern and glue them to either end. Onto these tape a little loop of cord for hanging the garland.

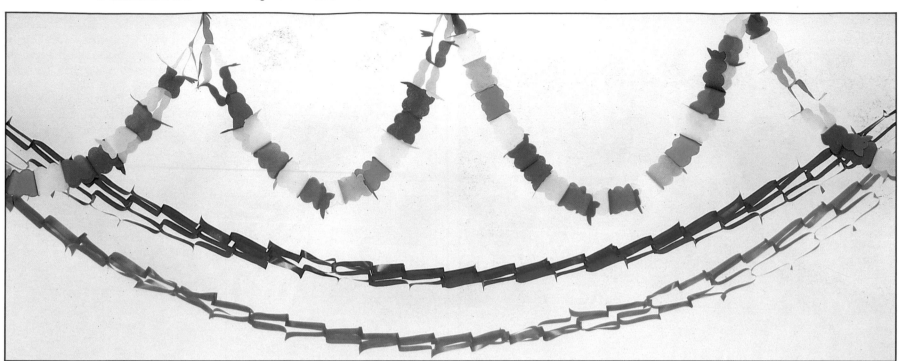

This variation on the standard pull-out chain is rectangular and has scalloped edges. It is very simple to make, though. Using the template on page 33, cut out lots of tissue shapes in different colours and mix them up for a random, multi-coloured effect.

All you need to do now is glue them together. Take the first two and stick them centre to centre.

Now take another piece and glue it to one of the first pieces at each end. Continue gluing, alternately centre-to-centre and end-to-end, until the chain is the required length.

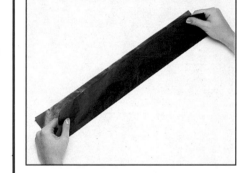

This traditional Christmas paper chain is easy to make and is shown cut from a waxed paper, which is stronger than ordinary tissue. First take a sheet of paper measuring about 50 by 35cm (20 by 14in) and fold it into four lengthwise.

Now make evenly spaced cuts all along one edge, stopping about 1.5cm (½in) from the other side. Turn the paper around and make additional cuts between the first set, again stopping short of the edge.

Open the chain out carefully. If you wish, you can glue the ends of two chains together to make a longer one. If your chain sags too much, string some thread through the top links to hold it together.

This is another fun way to hang up your Christmas cards. Simply take three long pieces of gift wrap or woven ribbon in red, green and gold, and plait them tightly together. Knot them at each end to hold them in place.

Now take some clothes pegs, lay them on several sheets of newspaper and spray them with gold paint. Turn them until all the sides have been covered and leave them to dry.

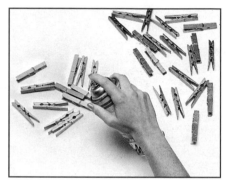

Hanging up your Christmas cards always poses a problem. Here is a simple way to overcome it while making an interesting 'picture' for your wall at the same time. First take a piece of wooden garden trellis, extend it, and spray it with gold paint.

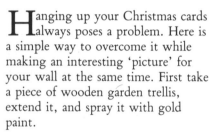

Fasten the ribbon to the wall at each end, and use the gold pegs to attach your Christmas cards to it. (If you prefer, and if you have some to spare, you could use tinsel instead of ribbon.)

While the trellis is drying, lay out some ordinary wooden clothes pegs and spray them gold as well. You will have to turn them over a few times so that all sides are covered.

When the trellis is dry, take some thick strands of tinsel and wind them all around the edge of the trellis to make a frame. Now hang the trellis on the wall, and use the pegs to attach the Christmas cards as they arrive.

Here is a lovely sparkly garland to hang at Christmastime. Cut Christmas tree and bell shapes from foil-covered cardboard, marking the shapes out first on the wrong side. Be careful when cutting as foil cardboard tends to crinkle at the edges.

Make a tiny hole in the top of each, using a hole punch, or the tip of a skewer. Using red twine, tie each shape to a long strand of tinsel, leaving even spaces between them. At the top of each bell, fix a bow of gold-covered wire; on the trees, a little star.

The paper used for these crackers is similar in texture to curling gift wrap ribbon and has a lovely shiny satin finish. Cover empty toilet paper rolls or cardboard tubes with white sticky-backed plastic, which prevents the colour from showing through. Now cut pieces of shiny paper, twice as long as the tubes, and wide enough to go easily around them.

Wrap the tube in the paper and fix in place with double-sided tape. Don't twist the ends; scrunch them in with elastic (rubber) bands, which you can then cover with strips of curling ribbon. Decorate the crackers with boiled sweets (hard candies), stuck on with double-sided tape. Staple the crackers onto a strip of tinsel and trim the garland with sweets and baubles.

Cut out a 38cm (15in) square of craft paper and mark a diagonal line between two corners. Then, using a pencil, string and compass, or drawing pin (thumbtack), draw an arc between the other two corners as shown. Cut along the arc. Fold the piece along the diagonal and use it to mark out two pieces of sticky-backed plastic. Add a 1.5cm (½in) border to one straight edge of black plastic.

Cut out the pieces. Peel off the backing and stick the white plastic into position on the paper. Do the same with the black, leaving the backing only on the border. Form a cone, remove the border backing and stick the edges of the cone together. Make two holes along the front join and insert red pom-poms. Secure the ends on the inside with tape.

Feel free to act the clown in this colourful hat. First of all, make a papier-mâché mould using a pudding basin (small mixing bowl) or plastic microwave dish. When it is fully dry, remove the mould and paint it with white emulsion (water-based) paint. Sand down any rough edges and give it a second coat of paint.

Make the 'hair' from red crepe paper — you will need about six layers of paper, stapled together along the top. Cut the paper into even strips, stopping about 2.5cm (1in) from the stapled edge.

Cut out a brim from light cardboard, allowing about 5cm (2in) for the brim itself and an extra 2.5cm (1in) on the inside for attaching the brim to the crown. Make triangular cuts around the inside of the brim, fold the triangles up and glue them to the inside of the hat. Decorate with a crepe paper band and large coloured spots. Finally, glue the hair to the inside of the hat.

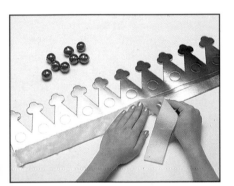

To make the crowns illustrated, we cheated a little by buying a pack of crown strips, which are available at some craft shops. In case you can't get them, there is a template on page 33. Cut out the crown in gold cardboard, first measuring the person's head for the length. Cut a strip of white fake fur 4.5cm (1¼in) wide, and fix this to the crown with double-sided tape.

Although a bit more complicated to make than a cardboard mask, this mask will last much longer. The face is made from papier-mâché and the mould is a balloon. Blow the balloon up as big as you can without bursting it, and build up the papier-mâché over at least one half. When it is dry, gently let the air out of the balloon by piercing the knotted end.

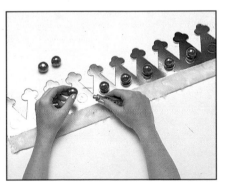

Above the fur glue fake jewels such as these painted wooden beads; if you can't get hold of any, large red sticky-backed spots will do. Now stick the two ends of the crown together with tape on the inside.

Trim the mask down, cutting the pointed end into a forehead. Cut out circular eyes and a curved mouth. Now give the mould a coat of white emulsion (water-based paint), sand it down and give it another two coats to make it as smooth a surface as possible.

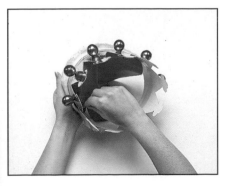

Finally, cut out a circle of red satin (draw around a large dinner plate). Put a strip of double-sided tape on the inside of the crown, and carefully pleat the satin onto it, shiny side up.

Around each eye paint four slightly triangular stripes. Also paint large red lips and cheeks on either side. For the nose, paint a ping pong ball red and glue it in place. For the hair, cut short lengths of yarn and attach them to strips of sticky tape; stick these to the back of the mask. Finally, take a piece of elastic, staple it to either side, and paint over the staples with a touch more emulsion.

For a stunning party mask, buy a ready-moulded mask from a stationer's or toy shop. The half-mask shown here is coloured with oil stencil pencils. Start with the pink; apply a little to a piece of waxed paper, then pick it up on the stencil brush. Using a circular motion, cover about half the mask. Repeat with the blue, filling in the gaps and giving the eyes a semblance of eyeliner.

Next take a short length of lace and glue it to the back of the top half of the mask, down to where the elastic is attached. Glue some strands of curling gift wrap ribbon on either side. (Curl the ribbon by running the blunt edge of a pair of scissor along it.) Lastly, glue some large sequins over the tops of the ribbons to hide the ends, and glue another one in the centre of the forehead.

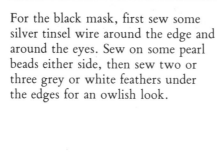

For the black mask, first sew some silver tinsel wire around the edge and around the eyes. Sew on some pearl beads either side, then sew two or three grey or white feathers under the edges for an owlish look.

This glamorous mask provides the perfect disguise this Christmas! Cut the basic shape from thin cardboard, using the template on the page opposite. Cover it with a fluorescent fabric, cut 1cm (½in) larger all round, clipping the edges as shown and also clipping through the eyeholes. Fold the borders over and stick them down on the reverse side.

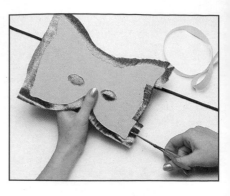

For the stick, cover a piece of garden cane with a strip of ribbon, and glue it in place. Wind fine tinsel or gold thread around it, and glue the ends down.

Cut a piece of gold foil paper to fit the back of the mask. Glue it down, first attaching the stick on one side. Decorate the front of the mask with sequins, feathers and pieces cut from a gold doily. If you can find only white ones in your local stores, spray a white one with gold paint.

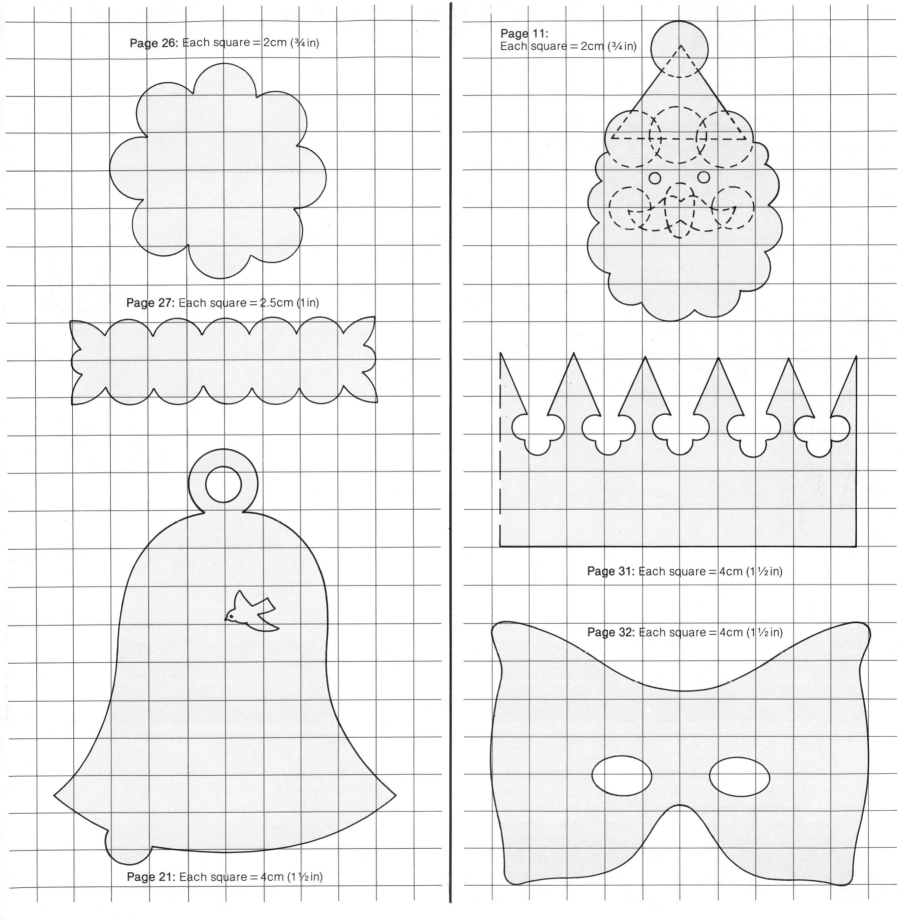

Page 26: Each square = 2cm (¾ in)

Page 11: Each square = 2cm (¾ in)

Page 27: Each square = 2.5cm (1 in)

Page 31: Each square = 4cm (1½ in)

Page 32: Each square = 4cm (1½ in)

Page 21: Each square = 4cm (1½ in)

Whether a children's party, a festive dinner party or the Christmas dinner itself, you can make the occasion a feast for the eyes as well as the palate by decorating the table with some of the stylish designs in this chapter. The centrepiece is the focal point of the table and, as such, is the most important feature. Here you will find an attractive range from which to choose, from sugared fruit and marzipan parcels to bowls of baubles and piles of mini crackers. Any of the eight beautiful napkin folds will also add style to the occasion, and most are quite easy to create. To complete each table setting, you can add some colourful name cards and present each guest with a personal gift.

Create a fully co-ordinated look for the table using traditional reds and greens. In this colourful setting, Christmas tree shapes are the prevailing theme, appearing in everything from the placemats (see page 40) to the cake. The gifts include traditional Christmas crackers (page 48) and a felt Christmas stocking containing a chocolate teddy bear (page 47) which can also double as a place marker.

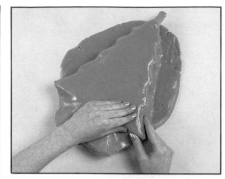

Carefully roll the sheet of icing over the rolling pin and unroll it onto the cake. Shape the icing around the cake, keeping your hands wet to smooth out any cracks.

Add rows of edible cake balls to suggest garlands draped across the tree.

Place tiny red ribbon bows on the cake. (You can use a glass-headed pin to secure the bows, but take care to remove them all before serving the cake.)

Place a selection of 'presents' around the bottom of the tree — the ones used here are Christmas tree decorations.

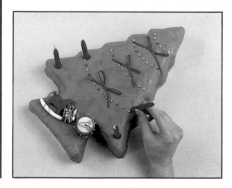

Push red wax candles into the icing around the edges of the tree to complete the effect.

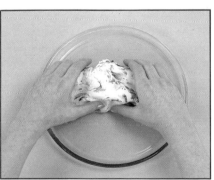

This festive Christmas tree cake will be the featured attraction at a Christmas tea. The cake can be made to your own traditional recipe and should be baked in a Christmas tree cake tin. The simplest method for icing the cake is to use ready-to-roll fondant icing. Knead the block into a ball and work in some green food colouring.

Roll the coloured icing out flat on a cool surface, first sprinkling some icing, or confectioner's, sugar on the worktop to prevent the icing from sticking.

A touch of gold gives this platter of fruit and nuts extra richness. Begin by spraying ivy, clementines, bay leaves and fir cones with gold paint. (If the fruit will be eaten, make sure that the paint you are using is non-toxic.)

T his centrepiece is very effective, but simple and long-lasting. If you or any of your friends have any plastic fruit that has been sitting around for some time and is ready to be thrown away, this is the perfect opportunity to give it a new lease of life. First take a deep plastic plate and spray it gold. Next take a paper doily and spray it gold also. When they are both dry, glue the doily to the plate.

Meanwhile, take a selection of plastic oranges, apples, bananas, grapes, etc., plus some fake ivy and some pine cones, and spray them either gold or bronze. Using both colours makes for variety. Let a little of their real colour come through; it adds interest. Wind the ivy around the edge of the plate, gluing it here and there to keep it in place.

Place the ivy leaves around the edge of a plain oval platter. The flatter the plate, the better, for this will allow the ivy leaves to hang over the edge.

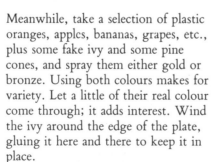

Now fill the middle with the fruit and pine cones. Again, you will have to dab a little glue here and there so that it withstands any movement.

Arrange the clementines on the platter, surround them with dates and nuts, and place a bunch of shiny black grapes on top. Add the gold leaves and fir cones for a luxurious finishing touch.

FROSTED FRUIT

GOLD AND SILVER CRACKERS

This stunning centrepiece looks grand enough to grace the most formal dinner party this Christmas, and yet is very simple to make. Using a pastry brush, coat each piece of fruit with egg white.

Working over a large plate, sprinkle granulated sugar over the fruit so that it adheres to the coating of egg. Alternatively, the fruit can be dipped into a bowl of sugar, although this tends to make the sugar lumpy.

Ivy leaves are used here to form a decorative border; but remember to use a doily to separate the poisonous leaves from the fruit if you intend to eat the fruit later.

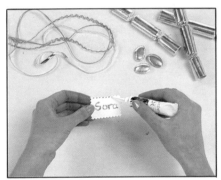

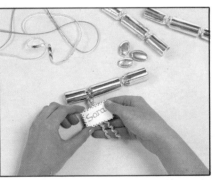

These attractive miniature crackers form an eye catching centrepiece, and the surrounding sweets make a delicious accompaniment to coffee at the end of the meal. For the name tags, cut small squares and rectangles from white cardboard. Trim the edges decoratively, then write the names and embellish the edges of the card with silver or gold paint.

Cut lengths of gold and silver ribbon or braid about 15cm (6in) long. Tie a ribbon around one end of each cracker. Dab a spot of glue on the back of each name tag and press it onto the ribbon.

Pile the crackers onto a large plate covered with a gold doily. Place those with name cards near the top of the pile. For a finishing touch, surround the pile of crackers with gold and silver dragées.

Clementines are a favourite at Christmas, and here an attractive effect has been created by hand-painting a plain wicker basket to match the colour of the fruit. Paint the basket inside and out with a water-based paint in the background colour, using a small decorating brush. Leave the basket to dry.

Exquisite marzipan fruits deserve special presentation. Nestling in little tissue 'parcels' and piled into a cake stand, they make a colourful centrepiece. All you need is several different colours of tissue paper and some pinking shears. Instead of marzipan fruits, you could use chocolates or marrons glacés.

Dip a sponge into a saucer containing the contrasting colour of paint. Dab the sponge a few times on a piece of scrap paper to remove any excess. Then sponge all over the outside of the basket, replenishing your paint supply when necessary.

From a double layer of one colour of tissue, cut a 10cm (4in) square. Pinking shears give an attractive serrated edge. From another colour of tissue, also double, cut a smaller square, measuring about 6cm (2½in).

Arrange the fruit in the basket as shown, adding a few leaves for contrast. Clementines are shown here, but apples, bananas and other fruit could be added for variety.

Lay the smaller square on top of the larger one. Place the marzipan fruit in the centre and gather the tissue around it. Hold it in place for a few seconds and then let go; the crumpled tissue will retain its rosette shape. Place several of the parcels on a doily-lined glass or china cake stand.

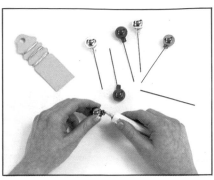

For a bright party centrepiece — ideal for Christmas or New Year's Eve — fill a glass bowl with a mixture of shiny glass baubles, foil crackers, feathers and streamers. To make clusters of small baubles, first remove the hanging string. Put a dab of glue inside the neck of each bauble and push in a short length of florist's wire. Leave them to dry.

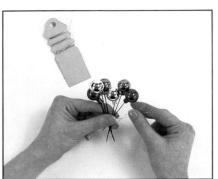

Hold the wired baubles in a cluster and wind fine fuse wire around the stems to hold them together.

Wrap a piece of shiny giftwrap ribbon around the stems and tie it into a bow. Arrange the baubles and other ornaments in the bowl as shown.

Believe it or not, this arrangement is quite simple once you get the hang of folding the cones. You need two colours of foil paper. Cut out lots of boat shapes 16.5cm (6½in) along the top and 12.5 (5in) along the bottom and about 6cm (2½in) deep. Glue one colour to another, back-to-back.

Form each boat into a cone and glue it in place. The first few you make may not look too professional, but it doesn't matter; these can go on the outside of the stand and will be partially covered. You will soon get the hang of folding the cones. Bend the bottoms under; it helps to hold the shape and looks tidier.

When you have several cones made, start gluing them around the edge of a 20cm- (8in-) diameter silver cake board. Place another two layers inside the first, leaving room for a chunky candle in the middle.

This sparkling placemat is an obvious winner for Christmas. First draw a Christmas tree on the reverse (matt) side of a piece of shiny green cardboard. The length should be about 10cm (4in) longer than the diameter of your dinner plate and the width about 20cm (8in) wider. Cut out the mat using a craft knife and a steel ruler.

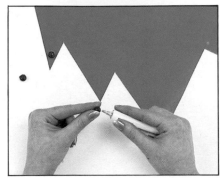

Add 'ornaments' by sticking tiny baubles to the tips of the tree using strong glue.

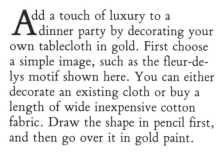

Add a touch of luxury to a dinner party by decorating your own tablecloth in gold. First choose a simple image, such as the fleur-de-lys motif shown here. You can either decorate an existing cloth or buy a length of wide inexpensive cotton fabric. Draw the shape in pencil first, and then go over it in gold paint.

Cut out or buy a star shape to put at the top of the tree. Finally, stick small silver stars over the mat. Or, if you prefer, just scatter the stars freely over the mat, first positioning each mat on the table.

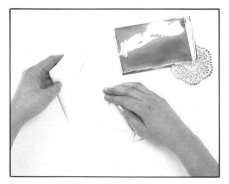

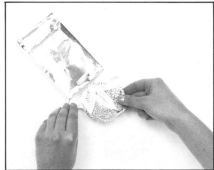

To echo the shape of the fleur-de-lys symbol you can dress up your table napkins as shown. A napkin with a lacy edge will look best. Fold the napkin into a square. Keeping the lacy edge nearest to you, fold the left- and right-hand corners in to overlap one another. Fold the remaining point in to meet them.

Slide the napkin, lacy edge towards you, into a shining foil gift bag. Because both napkin and china are white, a lacy gold coaster was inserted into the bag, underneath the lace detail on the napkin to give it more definition.

GOLDEN TOUCH

Give a touch of luxury to plain white china by using a larger gold plate underneath each dinner plate. You will need some old white china plates, about 1.5 to 2.5cm (½ to 1in) wider all around than your dinner plates, some ivy, holly and mistletoe, gold spray paint and a few gold or silver dragées.

Place the plate on a large sheet of scrap paper and spray it with gold paint, making sure that you follow the manufacturer's instructions on the can.

Lay the holly and ivy leaves on a sheet of scrap paper and coat them with gold paint. Leave them to dry for 10 to 15 minutes, and then arrange the painted leaves on the smaller white plate with an unsprayed sprig of mistletoe for contrast. Add a few silver dragées for the finishing touch.

TASSEL NAPKIN RING

This tasselled napkin ring will add a touch of class to the dinner table this Christmas. You will need two tassels and approximately 40cm (16in) of cord per napkin, and a strong fabric glue. Attach the tassels to the cord by wrapping the loop around the cord and pulling the tassels through it.

Make the ring by feeding the cord through both loops of the tassels twice more. Make sure that the ring is large enough to slip easily over the napkin.

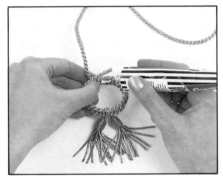

Using a strong glue, secure the ends of the cord to the back of the ring. Lay one end along the back and trim it. Having applied the glue to the inside of the ring as shown, wrap the remaining end over the cords, covering the trimmed end. Cut the remaining piece of cord on the inside, and clamp it in position until it is dry.

PURE ELEGANCE

DOUBLE JABOT

For best results use a crisply starched napkin to make this attractive fold. First fold the napkin lengthwise into three to form a long rectangle. Lay it horizontally with the free edge away from you, and fold the left- and right-hand ends in to meet in the centre.

Fold the napkin twice to form a square and position it with the loose corners at the top right. Fold the top corner back diagonally to meet the lower left corner, then turn it back on itself as shown. Continue to fold the corner back and forth to create a 'concertina' effect along the diagonal strip of napkin.

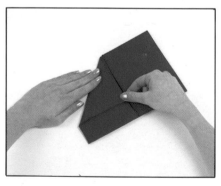

Fold down the top right- and left-hand corners to meet in the centre, forming a point. Take the napkin in both hands and flip it over towards you so that the point is facing you and the flat side of the napkin is uppermost.

Lift the next layer of fabric from the top right-hand corner and repeat the process described above to create two parallel strips with zigzag edges.

Lift the sides and pull them over towards one another to form a cone shape. Tuck the left-hand corner into the right-hand corner to secure it. Turn the napkin around and place it on a plate as shown in the main picture.

Pick the napkin up in both hands with the zigzag folds in the centre. Fold it in half diagonally to form a triangle, keeping the pleats on the outside. Take the right-hand and left-hand corners of the triangle and curl them back, tucking one into the other to secure them. Stand the napkin upright on a plate as shown.

Fold the napkin in half to form a crease along the centre line. Then open the napkin out again. Fold one half of the napkin lengthwise into three by bringing the top edge of the square inwards to the centre line and then folding it back on itself as shown. Repeat with the second half.

Fold the napkin in half lengthwise by tucking one half under the other along the centre line. Lay the resulting strip flat with the three folded edges facing you. Mark the centre of this strip with a finger and fold the right-hand edge in towards the centre and back on itself as shown. Repeat with the left-hand side.

A crisply starched napkin is required for this pretty fold. Lay the napkin flat. Fold two edges to meet in the centre as shown. Then fold the half nearest you across the centre line and over on the top of the other half, to form a long, thin rectangle.

Pull the top left-hand corner across towards the top right-hand corner to create a triangle, pressing down gently along the folds to hold them in place. Repeat with the remaining left-hand folds, and then do the same with all the right-hand folds. Ease the folds open slightly and display the napkin with the centre point facing the guest.

Fold the right-hand end of the rectangle in towards the centre, and with another fold double it back on itself as shown. Repeat with the left-hand side so that the double folds meet in the centre.

Pull the right-hand back corner across to the left, bringing the front edge across the centre line to form a triangle. Anchoring the right hand side of the triangle with one hand, use the other hand to fold the corner back to its original position, thus creating the 'wings' of the arrangement. Repeat the process on the left-hand side.

ORIENTAL FAN

PURE AND SIMPLE

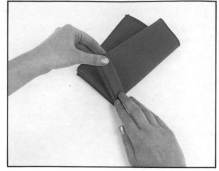

This elegant napkin fold is easier to produce than it looks. First fold the napkin in half diagonally, then bring the left- and right-hand corners up to meet at the apex.

This highly effective design benefits from a well-starched napkin and is very easy to make. Begin by folding the napkin in half lengthwise and then fold one end of the oblong backwards and forwards in concertina- or accordion-style folds, until just past the halfway point.

Holding the folds firmly together, fold the napkin lengthwise down the middle to bring both ends of the 'concertina' together. Keeping the folds in position in one hand, fold the loose flap of the napkin over across the diagonal.

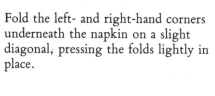

Turn the napkin over, and fold the lower corner up slightly as shown.

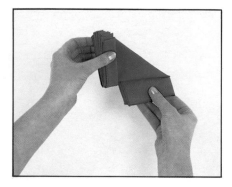

Push the flap underneath the support as shown to balance the napkin, and, letting go of the pleats, allow the fan to fall into position.

Fold the left- and right-hand corners underneath the napkin on a slight diagonal, pressing the folds lightly in place.

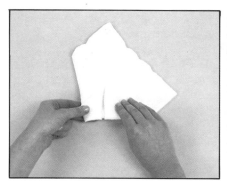

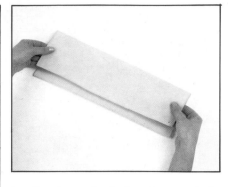

This design looks best in a conical glass but can be adapted for a wider-based container. Although it takes a little more practice than most, it is worth the effort. First lay the napkin flat and fold it in three lengthwise. Position it as shown, with the free edge on top.

Take hold of the top left-hand and right-hand corners of the napkin with the index finger and thumb of each hand. Roll the corners diagonally towards you as shown.

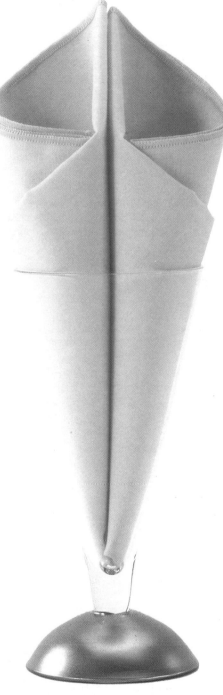

To make this graceful fold, lay the napkin flat and fold it in half diagonally to form a triangle. Position it with the folded edge towards you. Bring the top corner towards you, so that the point overlaps the folded edge slightly. Carefully turn the napkin over and repeat with the other corner.

Pleat the napkin evenly across from left to right, in accordion- or concertina-style, folds. Holding the straight edge of the 'concertina' firmly in position, arrange the napkin in a glass. Pull the front layer of the top point towards you, creating a pointed flap over the front of the glass.

Without releasing your hold on the napkin, continue to roll the corners inwards in one sweeping movement by swivelling both hands and napkin down, up and over until your hands are together palms uppermost. By now the napkin should be rolled into two adjacent flutes. Release your hands and place the napkin in a glass, arranging it neatly.

KITE PLACE CARDS

TARTAN PLACE CARD

These colourful place cards are perfect for a children's Christmas party. For each kite you will need stiff paper in two colours. From each colour cut two rectangles, each 10 by 15cm (4 by 6in). Draw a line down the centre, then another line at right angles across it, 5cm (2in) from one end. Join up the points, then cut off the four corners; set them aside.

Add a truly Scottish flavour this Christmas by making these tartan place cards for your guests. Use plaid ribbon and either white or coloured lightweight cardboard, and add a kilt pin for the finishing touch.

Use two of the corners of the red card to decorate the yellow kite, glueing them in place as shown. Similarly, use two of the leftover pieces of the yellow card to decorate the red kite. Write the name on each kite.

Cut a rectangle of cardboard about 10 by 12cm (4 by 5in), or a size to fit the plate. Fold it in half, and write the name on the left-hand side. Cut a piece of ribbon to edge the card front and back, allowing a little extra to turn under the edges.

Cut out squares of coloured tissue, allowing three for each kite. On the back of each kite, glue a 40cm (16in) strip of thin ribbon. Pinch the squares of tissue together in the centre and tie the ribbon around them. Cut a small strip of cardboard, fold it in two and glue it to the back of the kite; use this hook to attach the kite to a glass.

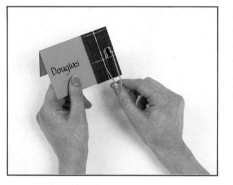

Stick ribbon onto the card with fabric glue, folding the excess underneath as shown. Pin the kilt pin through the ribbon and card to complete the authentically Scottish look.

Here's a novel way to show guests where to sit — a pastry place marker shaped like a Christmas tree. Make the dough by mixing three parts of white flour to one of salt, a spoonful of glycerine and enough cold water to give a good consistency. Knead the pastry for about 10 minutes, then roll it flat on a floured surface.

Cut out the shapes with a sharp knife or a pastry cutter. Remember to make a hole for the ribbon. Bake the pastry in the normal way.

Either leave the shapes plain or colour them with water-based paint. You can pipe your guests' names on using tube paint. Varnish the shapes (optional) and attach a ribbon. Note that these pastry shapes are not edible and should be used only for decorative purposes; however, they will keep for years. They can also be used as Christmas tree ornaments.

For a children's party at Christmas this ingenious place marker is sure to be a winner. First, cut two boot shapes from bright-coloured felt, making sure that they are large enough to enclose a chocolate teddy or other favour. Stick the shapes together with fabric glue, leaving the top open.

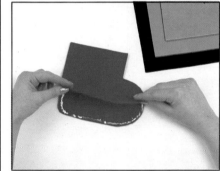

From contrasting felt, cut a zigzag strip for the upper edge and some letters to make the name.

Glue the strip and the letters to the boot as shown. Finally, insert the chocolate teddy into the boot.

Crepe paper

Tissue paper

Cardboard cylinder

Stiff paper

Gather the paper together at one end and tie it with ribbon. Leave the other end open to drop in the gift, hat and joke of your choice. Tie this end and trim the ribbons neatly.

Cut a zigzag edge in the paper at both ends; or leave the ends plain, if you prefer.

Crackers are always a must at the dinner table at Christmas. The diagram above shows the materials required for a cracker: crepe paper for the outside, tissue paper for the lining, and stiff paper and a cardboard cylinder to hold the cracker in shape.

Cut the paper layers as indicated above. Roll them around the tube, and stick them in place securely with either glue or tape. A friction strip can be placed between the stiff paper and cylinder to provide a 'bang' when the cracker is pulled.

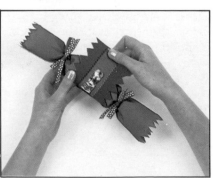

Add the final decorative touches — in this case, contrasting layers of crepe paper and a paper motif.

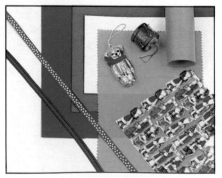

RED HOT CRACKERS

VICTORIAN CRACKER

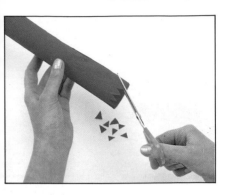

Stylish black and white paper decorates these modern bright red crackers. Follow the instructions on the page opposite for assembling the basic cracker, using red crepe paper for the outer layer. Cut a decorative edging, if desired, at both ends.

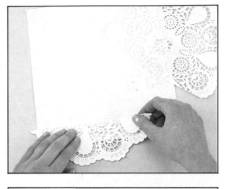

This old-fashioned cracker makes a charming addition to the table. Follow the basic step-by-step guide for making a cracker on the page opposite, cutting the outer crepe paper layer 5cm (2in) short of the recommended size. Make up the difference by attaching strips of paper doilies as shown, using double-sided tape or glue to secure the strips at each end.

Cut a rectangular piece of black and white gift wrap or other patterned paper, long enough to go around the cylinder with a small overlap. Cut the long edges to match the ends of the cracker. Wrap the strip around the cracker and glue along the join.

Cover the join of doily and crepe paper at one end with a length of ribbon in a contrasting colour, tied in a bow. Insert the chosen motto and small gifts in the cylinder. Tie the other end as before, and trim the ribbon ends neatly.

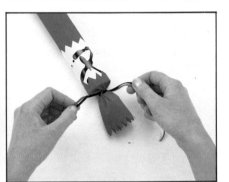

Tie one end with two lengths of fine ribbon in black, white and/or red. Insert the gift into the cylinder and tie the other end. Add place cards or write names on the crackers if appropriate.

Cut out a traditional Victorian scrap or motif from an old Christmas card or other greeting card, and glue it to the cracker. Alternatively, you may be able to purchase attractive Victorian-style motifs from a stationer's.

GIFT BOX POM-POM

SQUARE GIFT BOX

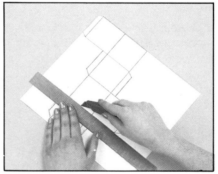

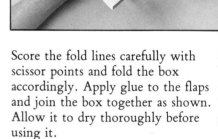

Little boxes, decorated with tissue paper pom-poms and filled with candies, make lovely gifts at the Christmas table. To make the pom-pom, fold some tissue paper to get at least 12 layers, measuring 7cm (3in) square. Using a cup or glass, mark a circle on the paper, and cut it out. Staple the layers together at the centre.

Cut strips into the centre, making them about 5mm (¼in) wide at the edge and stopping short of the staple. Fluff up the tissue paper to form a pom-pom, and glue it to the box. To make the box, copy the template below and then refer to the instructions adjacent (i.e. those for the square gift box).

This elegant little box is ideal for wrapping a special gift for each of your dinner guests this Christmas. First draw the diagram to the specified measurements, then trace it. Tape the tracing to the wrong side of medium-weight cardboard with masking tape and draw over the outline to make a light indentation in the cardboard. Cut around the outline.

Score the fold lines carefully with scissor points and fold the box accordingly. Apply glue to the flaps and join the box together as shown. Allow it to dry thoroughly before using it.

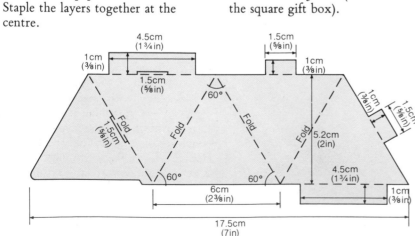

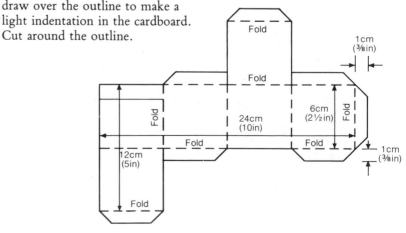

Give each of your guests a little table gift this Christmas, wrapped up in some pretty fabric. Fine scented soap makes a perfect gift for the ladies. Cut a 15cm (6in) square of fabric, using pinking shears for a decorative edge and to prevent fraying.

For a gift bag, place the soap in the centre of the square of fabric. Gather the corners together in the centre. Tie a contrasting ribbon around the fabric and into a bow. For an envelope, fold the four corners of the square over the soap to overlap in the centre.

A stunning, yet simple, idea for a festive dinner party, these net bags contain sweets for your guests. Cut a large gold doily in half. Fold the edges around to meet one another, creating a cone shape, and then secure them with tape.

Hold the flaps of the envelope in place and tie them up with a contrasting ribbon. Finish off with a large bow.

Cut out a square of black dress-maker's or milliner's net. Use it double for a fuller effect. Holding the net square in one hand, place the gold doily cone into it. Place three or four black and gold dragées in the cone.

Gather the net and doily cone into a 'waist', leaving some extra at the top. Secure it with sewing thread, wrapped tightly around it several times, or with an elastic band. Cut equal lengths of thin gold and black ribbon, and tie them around the waist and into a bow at the front.

FESTIVE FLORAL DESIGNS

For those who prefer more natural Christmas decorations flowers are a must, providing all the colour and festive splendour anyone could want. Fresh flowers are glorious but dried flowers are so much more durable — surviving the whole festive season and on to the next! And, as this chapter shows, dried flowers are so versatile, ideal for decorating anything from wreaths and centrepieces to coasters and candlestick holders. To help you identify the plants used, a list of both common and Latin names has been provided on page 96.

Most arrangements are supported by either florists' foam or wire mesh. The foam comes in two forms — one for fresh flowers (designed to absorb water), the other for dried flowers. The latter comes in several shapes and sizes — spheres, blocks and cones — and can be cut down to any size required. Dry moss is also used as a support — packed inside a wire mesh frame to form a solid 'cushion' or bound on to a wreath frame with reel wire. Other than these supports, you will also need a sharp knife, a strong pair of scissors or secateurs and, for the dried flowers, some wire — stub wires (which come in various lengths and thicknesses), black reel wire and silver rose wire.

WIRING TECHNIQUES

Some dried flowers — yarrow and larkspur for example — have strong, firm stems that need no support. Others, such as helichrysums, have weak stems that cannot withstand the weight of the flowerheads. In the latter case, wire can be used to support the flower. Cut a stem down to about 4cm (1½in) and place it against the end of a stub wire. Then bind the length of the stem to the wire using silver reel wire.

To increase the impact of colours in a display, flowers are frequently tied into small bunches before they are arranged. To do this, cut down the stems of two or three flowers — weak stems should be cut down to about 4cm (1½in); strong ones can be left longer. Take a length of stub wire and bend back the top 3-4cm (1-1½in) to form a hair-pin shape. Place the pin against the end of the stems, bent end towards the flowerheads. Then, starting about half way down the pin, begin to wind the long end of the wire around both the stems and the short end of the wire. Bind it about three times as shown below, then straighten it so that it forms a 'stem'. Trim the wire to the required length and insert it into the display.

To give flowers more impact in a display, wire them into small bunches before arranging them. First bend the end of a stub wire to form a hair-pin shape.

Cut the flower stems short and place them against the pin. Wind the long end of wire round about three times then straighten it to make a 'stem'.

Transfuse the atmosphere this Christmas with the sweet scent of lavender and pot-pourri by making this charming basket. Begin by wiring small bunches of lavender — about three to four stems each. Attach a bunch to the rim of the basket, wrapping the wire through the wicker work. Position the next bunch over the stems of the first to cover the wires. Continue round the rim.

A collection of brilliantly coloured flowers makes a striking display for the sideboard. Begin by moulding some wire mesh into a three-dimensional shape, keeping the base flat and the top end open. Pack the mesh with dry moss, then close up the open end. Now insert wired bunches of stirlingia — tall, upright stems at the top, shorter, horizontal ones lower down.

When the rim is fully covered, cover the handle in the same way. Add a splash of colour to the display with wired bunches of small red helichrysum (everlasting or strawflower). Attach them at intervals to the rim of the basket, using the same method as before. Put two more bunches on the handle.

Next, arrange a few stems of blue larkspur around the top, and shorter bunches of blue statice lower down, following the general pattern set by the stirlingia. Follow with wired bunches of pink-dyed quaking grass, breaking out of the outline, and a few clumps of blue-dyed *Leucodendron brunia*.

Make a single bow out of deep red ribbon and wire it on to the middle of the handle. Cover the wire with a strand of lavender, fixing it in place using fine silver rose wire. To finish, fill the basket with pot-pourri, choosing a type that complements the colours of the arrangement.

Once you are happy with the general shape of the arrangement, start to fill in with bunches of large pink helichrysum (strawflower or everlasting). Pack them deep into the display. Add bright yellow highlights next with bunches of cluster-flowered helichrysum.

Finally, wire together a few bunches of rich red roses and scatter them throughout the display. It is important to position the roses last, because this ensures that the heads remain well exposed.

An attractive winter's wreath in muted creams and golds makes a pleasant change from the usual seasonal reds and greens, and gives a different and stylish Christmas decoration. Begin by covering a wreath ring in moss, packing the dry moss around the frame and binding it firmly in place with black reel wire.

Wire together some clumps of cream sea lavender and virtually cover the entire ring with it. Next, take some purple statice and wire together several bunches.

Intersperse the purple statice evenly amongst the cream coloured flowers which form the base of the garland. Then, place at regular intervals some wired clumps of yarrow and rhodanthe (sunray).

Finally, gather about 10 to 12 cones and wire them together in a large bunch. With more wire fix the cones to the wreath at the front. Pull a few strands of the flowers between the cones to add contrast. Intersperse a few more cones throughout the wreath as shown to complete the picture. This combination of flowers and cones is remarkably inexpensive, yet the result is quite stunning.

Hang this brilliant golden wreath on your front door this Yuletide to provide a colourful welcome for all your guests. It is possible to make your own base for the wreath as described opposite, but a florist should be able to provide you with a sturdy woven cane base, such as this one, for a small cost.

Wire up plenty of colourful flowers, either singly or in bunches, depending on their size. Allow plenty of wire for attaching them securely to the base. The flowers used here include helichrysum (strawflowers or everlasting), yarrow and sea lavender.

Pine cones can easily be wired around the base. Choose small closed ones for the best effect. If you cannot collect the cones yourself, your florist or a shop selling dried flowers will probably have some, and they should cost very little.

Some dried flowers come ready-wired, which makes the work easier, but a little more expensive. When everything is ready, begin wiring the various items onto the base, laying them all in the same direction.

Some flower heads will be very delicate and break off. If so, simply dab a little glue on the back and stick them on. If you start to run out of dried flowers, or you want to save some money, heather from the garden can be included; it will dry naturally once it is in place.

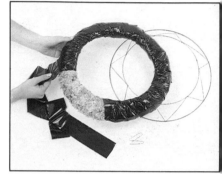

This stunning wreath, with its wealth of contrasting colours and materials, makes a beautiful decoration to hang on the door during the festive season. Begin by making a base using a wire wreath frame and some dry moss, binding the moss firmly on to the frame with black reel wire. Cover the base with green wreath wrap.

Take some colourful fabric and cut it up into rectangles. Now wrap about 8 to 10 small foam spheres in the fabric, gathering the material at the top and securing with wire. Leave long wire 'tails' for attaching the balls to the frame. Position the spheres in groups of two or three at regular intervals around the wreath.

Wire clumps of green amaranthus (love-lies-bleeding) and insert them into the wreath, keeping them generally quite close to the fabric spheres.

Next, wire clumps of white larkspur and intersperse these amongst the amaranthus. These reflect the white in the fabric and add highlights to the arrangement. Wire together several groups of cones and place them standing upright in the arrangement so that they do not get lost among the other plants.

Soften the display by scattering bunches of soft pink rabbit's or hare's tail grass throughout. The seeds tend to moult very easily so be careful when wiring and inserting the grass not to overhandle it.

Pick out the colours in the fabric by dotting clumps of rust coloured nipplewort (or broom bloom) throughout. The dark tones will also add depth to the display.

Finish off with a few colourful satin bows, binding each bow together with wire rather than actually tying it. Insert the bows in amongst the fabric spheres, trailing the tails prettily over the arrangement.

This striking tartan wreath makes a charming centrepiece for the table at Christmas and New Year. First you will need to buy a twig ring from a florist. Begin by individually wiring several heads of red rose. Arrange these in three small groups, evenly spaced around the ring.

Next, wire together nine small bunches of anaphalis (pearl everlasting) and push them into the ring so that they surround the roses. Take three lengths of tartan ribbon and make three single bows, wiring them together rather than actually tying them.

Take a fourth piece of ribbon, fold it in half and push a piece of wire through the folded end: this will form the long 'tails' of the arrangement. Cut a 'V' shape in the ends of the ribbons to finish them neatly, then wire a bow into each of the three gaps between the flowers. To complete the picture, wire the tartan tails beneath one of the bows.

Add several sprigs of holly, again securing them with wire. If the holly is a bit short of berries, you can add some fake berries at this point.

To hang the wreath you will need two lengths of satin ribbon. Each piece should be twice the length of the drop from the ceiling to your hanging height, plus an extra 20cm (8in) for tying around the wreath. Tie each of the four ends opposite one another around the wreath so that the two lengths cross in the centre.

Make four bows from the same colour ribbon and pin them to the wreath over the four tying-on points.

T his festive wreath makes an ideal centrepiece if you're short of space on the table — it can be suspended from a hook screwed into the ceiling. Use wire cutters to snip the hook off a coat hanger. Bend the hanger into a circular shape. Bunch damp sphagnum moss around the wire, binding black reel wire or gardener's wire around it to hold it in place.

Take several bushy branches of evergreen, such as cypress, and arrange them to cover the circlet of moss, overlapping the pieces to cover any stalks. Tie the branches to the ring with wire.

Gently push a length of florist's wire through each of four red wax candles, approximately 1.5cm (½in) above the bases, as shown.

Position each candle halfway between two bows, and twist the wire around the wreath to hold it in place. To hang the wreath, tie another length of ribbon around the two main ribbons where they cross, make a loop to go over the hook, and tie the ends in a bow.

WARM WELCOME

A traditional wreath on the front door gives a warm welcome to Christmastime callers. To begin, take a wire coat hanger and pull it into a circle. Bend the hook down to form a loop.

Now wire together small bunches of holly, spruce and other foliage. Then attach each bunch to the circle. Be careful when handling the holly; you can get a bit scratched, and some people can come out in a rash from it. Keep going in one direction until the whole circle is covered.

On top of this add some wired pine cones and, for extra colour, some curly red ribbon. (Use curling gift wrap ribbon for this, running the blunt edge of a pair of scissors along it to make it curl.) Red holly berries look great if you can get hold of them, but they tend to drop very quickly, so they would need replacing often. Finish off with a big red satin bow.

CANDLE CENTREPIECE

This sort of arrangement always looks very hard to achieve, but in fact it is very simple, provided you assemble everything you need before starting. What you need is a ring of florists' foam with a plastic base, which you can get from a florist. Also buy three plastic candle holders; stick these into the foam.

You will need holly, ivy and fern, all of them either real or fake, plus a selection of dried flowers. Used here are daisy-like sunrays, yellow helichrysum (strawflowers or everlasting), yarrow, safflowers and sea lavender. Simply break pieces off these and stick them into the foam. Try to space the flowers evenly in between the foliage.

When you have finished, stick three candles into the holders already placed. If any of the foliage is real, make sure to keep the foam damp.

This elegant candle-ring is the ideal centrepiece for a festive dinner party but it will only remain fresh for the one occasion. A circular cake base serves as the foundation for the arrangement. Begin by attaching strands of ivy to the edge of the base, securing them with drawing pins.

The sideboard, as well as the table, needs a little dressing up at Christmas. This is bright and cheery, and the materials are quite easy to get hold of. If you don't have woodland nearby your florist should have small sections of bark for sale. Also buy a plastic candle holder. Onto the bark first put a large lump of green Plasticine (modelling clay), and on the top stick your candle holder.

Build up the ring by adding more strands and bunches of leaves until only a small space remains in the centre. Push stems of freesia among the ivy leaves to provide colour contrast.

Now take some plastic or silk fern and spray it gold. Break off pieces when it is dry, and stick them into the Plasticine. Also wire up strands of red paper ribbon, pine cones and red baubles and stick these in.

Use a mixture of white and green candles of varying heights to form the centre of the arrangement. Secure each candle to the base with a blob of glue or Plasticine (modelling clay).

When the Plasticine is artistically concealed, pop a red candle in the holder, and set the arrangement on the sideboard. Put a mat under it, though, or it will scratch the surface.

Add style to the dinner table with this traditional red and green centrepiece. Take a flat circular base — a cork mat or cake base will do — and glue single ruscus leaves around the edge. Stick three blocks of florists' foam on top, keeping one taller than the others. Now insert the red candles into the foam, cutting them down as necessary to vary their heights.

Build up the arrangement using gold-sprayed poppy heads, white helichrysum (strawflower or everlasting) and more ruscus leaves. The white adds essential highlights to the arrangement. Finish off by scattering single red roses throughout the display.

This attractive 'woodland' design makes the perfect centrepiece for those wishing to create a more rustic effect this Christmas. Begin by making a base out of three large dried leaves, such as these cobra leaves. Glue the leaves together, then glue a block of florists' foam on top. Wire up several cones and walnuts, forcing the wire through the base of the nuts as far as it will go.

Wire together clumps of oak leaves and build up the outline of the display. Now insert the nuts and cones, placing the former in small groups. Keep the shape irregular to make it more interesting. Brighten the display by scattering small clumps of ammobium (sandflower) throughout. To finish, trim a candle to the required length and push it firmly into the foam.

To make this splendid Christmas centrepiece, take a flat circular base such as a cake board and glue a cone of florists' foam to the centre. Then glue or staple a length of gold netting round the edge of the base, gathering it into bunches as you go. Crumple lengths of red fabric or ribbon into double loops and wire the ends. Arrange them in a ring on top of the gold.

Spray a number of Chinese lanterns and lotus seedheads with gold paint. When they are dry, wire the ends and insert them evenly spaced into the cone. Intersperse several long-eared pods throughout, pushing · them deep into the arrangement. Add highlights with a few honesty seedheads (silver dollar plant). Then wire together bunches of small red helichrysum (strawflower or everlasting) and dot them among the other plants, adding colour throughout. Finish off by inserting a few groups of white leaf skeletons — about two to three leaves per group.

A pair of candlestick holders is transformed by a tightly-packed arrangement of dried flowers. For each stick, cut a sphere of florist's foam in half and hollow out the centre of each piece so that the foam sits snugly round the stem. Wrap a piece of florists' tape around the two halves to hold them together.

Create some pretty coasters using a few flowers and some mother-of-pearl discs. The latter can be bought from any shop specializing in shells. They should measure at least 4cm (1½in) more than the diameter of your glass base. Choose any combination of flowers or seedheads — shown above are helichrysum, honesty and hydrangea. Cut the heads off the plants.

Push short stems of orange South African daisy (a form of helichrysum) into the foam, keeping the arrangement spherical. Then fill in with small wired clumps of red helichrysum (strawflower or everlasting) and pink miniature sunray, being sure not to leave any gaps.

Now create a ring around the edge of a shell by gluing the heads in position. The honesty can be stuck down first — the heads slightly overlapping — and the red helichrysum can be glued down on top at regular intervals. If you are only using helichrysum, alternate the colours for a more interesting effect.

An old topper, bursting with colour, makes a delightfully unconventional design for the festive season. Begin by putting a large brick of soaked florists' foam into a container which will fit comfortably into the hat. Fan out sprays of *Mallalika* foliage and fill in with September flowers (a form of aster).

Rich red holly berries add a brilliant splash of colour to this attractive festive arrangement. Choose a long shallow glass bowl and pack it with wire mesh. Crushed wire mesh is the best medium for this type of shallow bowl as it keeps the flowers from sagging.

Recess white spray chrysanthemums into the foliage and use longer stems to establish the height towards the back. Have a couple trailing over the brim of the hat alongside a few of the September flowers.

Fill mesh with variegated *Pittosporum*, a bushy foliage which maintains its fullness even when cut short. Stems of gypsophilia (also known as baby's breath in the United States) are added next, spread across the arrangement.

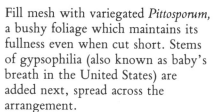

The focal point of the arrangement is poinsettia flowers which should be conditioned first by searing the stem ends with a lighted candle. fill in the outline and balance the display with deep red spray carnations.

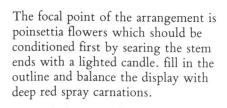

The three main stems of yellow lily, straddling the length of the vase, form the focal point. Intersperse the whole display with holly (known more specifically as English holly in the United States) berries, retaining the longer twigs for contrast and balance.

Keep the champagne in the refrigerator this Christmas and use the ice bucket for red roses instead! First, put soaked florists' foam at the base of the bucket. Then insert some variegated foliage — shown here is a spineless form of holly. Intersperse this with eight or nine red roses, still in bud. Have two or three longer stems rising from the foliage to one side at the back.

Fill in all the available space with jonquil, following the outline. The gold is highlighted by the yellow-edged foliage. (A handy tip: the roses will last longer if the stems are placed in boiling water for a minute before being given a long drink.)

Here, a wicker waste-paper basket forms the basis of an attractive festive arrangement of ferns and carnations. If you don't have a suitable red basket, you can spray a natural coloured one with red paint. Begin by taping soaked florists' foam into a container and positioning it inside the basket. Then fan out the fern fronds to form the setting for the flowers.

Take white spray carnations and intersperse them among the shorter fern fronds at the front, placing a few longer stems towards the back. Do the same with the bright red carnations.

Finish off by adding a sprinkling of September flowers (a form of aster) to soften the whole effect. (This display can also be acheived by pushing tiny phials of flowers into the soil of a real fern, such an arrangement being known as a pot-et-fleurs.

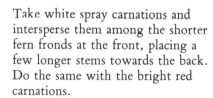

Add richness and colour to the home during the festive season with this vibrant design. First, roll some wire mesh into a tube, pack it with dry moss and close the ends. Squash the base into the basket and wire it in place as shown. Begin to form the outline of the arrangement with bleached white helichrysum (strawflower or everlasting), creating a dome shape.

Continue to build up the shape with white proteus. Add some clubrush next, followed by a number of cones, such as these meridianum. The colour of these two plants cleverly picks up the brown in the basket.

Wood always provides a perfect setting for dried flowers, and an old wooden plane makes an unusual festive design. Cut a block of florists' foam and wedge it tightly into the hole. Arrange wired clumps of cluster-flowered sunray first, keeping the outline low. Follow with pink *Leucodendron brunia,* allowing it to break out of the shape and dangle low over the sides.

Now add interest and a dash of colour with a few stems of bottlebrush. Put them in singly and keep them short so that their rich colour lies deep within the arrangement.

Complete the display with bright yellow clumps of cressia and cluster-flowered helichrysum. Place them low down in the arrangement, filling in the gaps between the other plants.

Soften the effect with a few clumps of grass interspersed throughout. To finish, add contrasting texture with three or four heads of *Leucodendron plumosum* set deep into the display.

To make a change from the more traditional holly, decorate your picture frames with this stunning tartan design. Cut a slice of florists' foam to fit one corner of the frame and tape it in place. Begin to loosely build up the shape using single stems of clubrush.

Add a splash of colour throughout the display with bright yellow cressia, allowing some to trail across the frame and picture. Then insert a number of single stems of bottlebrush to add interest and colour.

Fill out the display with plenty of bottlebrush foliage. Then add highlights with a few white leaf skeletons such as these peepal leaves.

Finally, make a double bow out of tartan ribbon, wiring it together rather than tying it. Attach this to the lower portion of the arrangement so that the long tails of the bow trail across the frame. Repeat the whole procedure on the opposite corner, being sure to keep the design well balanced.

WINTER SOLSTICE

The framework of this seasonal garland is made of cones and walnuts. Wire the cones by wrapping stub wire around the base. For the walnuts, push stub wire through one end as far as it will go. Take a group of cones and nuts and twist the wires together. Add to the base of the group and twist the wires again to secure. Continue in this way until the garland is long enough.

Wire together a double bow made from gold gift wrap ribbon and wire two extra tails on to it. (Just fold a length of ribbon in half for the tails and wire in the middle.) Attach the bow to one end of the garland, then wire a long length of ribbon to the same end. Wrap this through the garland, twisting it round the cones. Leave a long tail at the far end.

To finish, wire together small groups of bright Chinese lanterns and bunches of quaking grass. Intersperse them amongst the cones, entangling the wires to secure them.

FESTIVE MINIATURES

These miniature arrangements make pretty novelties to hang on the Christmas tree. One of them is made with cinnamon sticks. Take about three sticks and bind them together with wire. Wire on a double bow made out of gold gift wrap ribbon and then add a posy of cones and small red helichrysum (strawflower or everlasting).

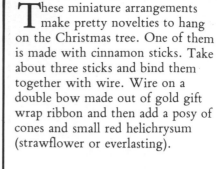

To make the other arrangement, first spray a small basket and some walnuts with gold paint. When these are dry, fill the basket with a block of florists' foam. Pack the foam with gold coloured South African daisies (a type of helichrysum) to form a spherical shape.

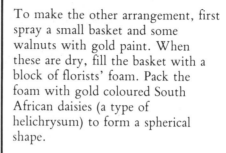

Push a length of wire through one end of each of the walnuts. Insert three or four nuts into the display, pushing them deep down amongst the flowers. Wire a small bow and attach it to the handle. Finally, hang each arrangement by means of a loop of gold cord.

Here are two more colourful decorations to hang on the Christmas tree. For the red ball, take a length of cord and wire the ends together, forming a loop. Push the wire right the way through a sphere of florists' foam and double it back on itself — into the foam — to secure. Now cover the foam with flowers.

Pack the flowers tightly into the foam to maintain the spherical shape. Those used here are deep red helichrysum (strawflower or everlasting). Fill in with little clumps of red nipplewort (or broom bloom). To finish, gather up and wire small pieces of silver netting, then insert them amongst the flowers.

This pretty display, arranged in a tiny gift box, makes an attractive miniature decoration. It would also make a delightful present. And with all that lavender, it smells as lovely as it looks. First cut a small block of florists' foam and pop it inside the box. Then wire a couple of red ribbons into bows.

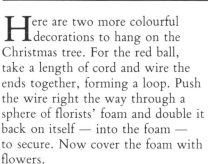

For this design wire together a few flowers, such as these small white helichrysum and blue-dyed *Leucodendron brunia,* and attach three decorative bells. Gather up a piece of red netting and bind it on to the flowers. Make a double red bow, tie a long piece of ribbon round the middle (by which to hang the decoration) and attach the bow to the netting with wire.

Wire together bunches of lavender and pack them into the foam, keeping the arrangement tallest in the middle and splaying it out at the sides. Now scatter tiny, daisy-like glixia or grass daisies throughout; push some deep into the display. Finish off by attaching the two red bows, one to the box, the other higher up on a stem of lavender.

A beautifully wrapped gift is a pleasure to give and a pleasure to receive. So here are over 40 imaginative ways to make your Christmas presents look that extra bit special. Having been shown how to wrap a variety of shapes, you will find some simple ways to make your own wrapping paper — a great cost saver — and lots of pretty decorations such as ribbon ties, rosettes and pom-poms to add those all-important finishing touches. There are also some ingenious ideas for disguising gifts: bottles become pencils; records – kites; books – playing cards. And finally, lots of inexpensive ways to make your own gift tags using last year's cards or motifs cut from wrapping paper.

Sometimes the gift wrap seems almost as expensive as the gift itself. But there are plenty of ways to get stylish results without the expense. Reels of gift ribbon can be turned into a vast array of different decorations, from stunning rosettes you couldn't tell apart from shop-bought versions to pretty pom-poms and posies. Braid, cord and even candies can also be used to make gifts that extra bit special.

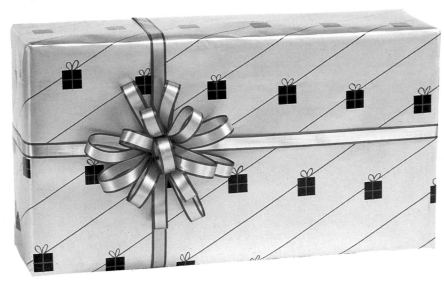

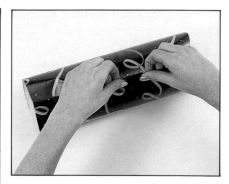

When wrapping a cylinder, avoid using very thick or textured paper as it will be difficult to fold neatly. Cut the paper longer than the cylinder, allowing for extra paper at each end to cover half the cylinder's diameter, and just wider than the gift's circumference. Roll the paper around the parcel and secure with a little tape.

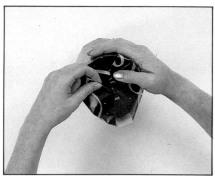

Begin folding the ends of the paper in a series of small triangles as shown here. Continue around the whole circumference, making sure that the 'triangles' are neatly folded into the centre.

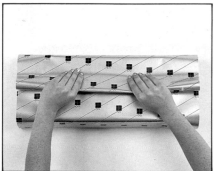

Wrapping square or rectangular presents isn't difficult — but perhaps your technique needs brushing up. Wrap the gift wrap tightly around the box. You can simply stick down the free edge with tape or, for a smarter effect, fold over the top edge of the paper and stick double-sided tape underneath it, leaving a neat fold visible at the join.

Use a single piece of tape at the centre to fix all the folds in place. If the finished folds are not even, you could cheat a little by sticking a circle of matching gift wrap over each end of the cylinder.

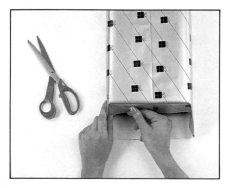

If your paper has a linear design, try to align the design so that the join is not too obvious. Fold the joined section of paper down over the end of the box to make a flap; crease the fold neatly. Trim off any excess paper so there is no unnecessary bulk.

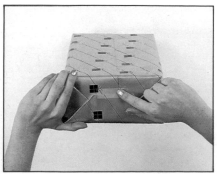

Crease the side flaps firmly, and fold them over the ends of the gift. Smoothing your hand along the side of the box and round on to the end ensures that each flap fits tightly. Fold up the remaining triangular flap, pulling it firmly along the edge of the box, and stick down; use invisible tape (its matt surface is scarcely discernible) or double-sided for the best results.

WRAPPING A SPHERE

AWKWARD ANGLES

The usual method of wrapping a sphere is to gather the paper around the gift and bunch it all together at the top. Here is a more stylish method. Put your circular gift in the centre of a square of paper, checking that the two sides of paper just meet at the top when wrapped around the gift. Cut off the corners of the square to form a circle of paper.

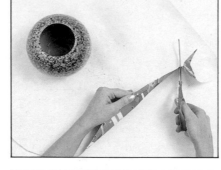

Bring one section of the paper to the top of the gift and begin to pleat it to fit the object as shown. The paper pleats at the top of the gift will end up at more or less the same point; hold them in place every three or four pleats with a tiny piece of sticky tape.

Continue pleating neatly and tightly all the way round the circle. It isn't as complicated or as time-consuming as it sounds once you've got the knack! When you have finished, the pile of pleats on top of the gift should look small and neat. Then you can either cover them with a small circle of paper stuck in place or, more attractively, add a bunch of colourful ribbons.

Wrapping awkwardly-shaped presents is just that — awkward. The gift wrap always looks creased and untidy around the angles of the gift. The solution is not to use paper — instead, use brightly-coloured cellophane which doesn't crumple. Cut a square of cellophane a great deal larger than your gift.

Gather the cellophane up and tie it into a bunch above the present. Fan out the excess and add some curled ribbon as a finishing touch. Alternatively, if your gift is cylindrical, roll it in cellophane somewhat longer than the parcel and gather the ends with ribbon.

Glittering wrapping paper is always glamorous, and with glitter available in such a variety of colours your creativity need know no bounds! Spread out a sheet of plain coloured paper and, using a bottle of glue with a fine nozzle, draw a series of simple patterns across it.

Sprinkle a line of glitter across the paper. Tip up the sheet and gently shake all the glitter from one side of the paper to the other, across the glued designs, making sure that all the patterns have been well covered. Tip the excess glitter off the page on to a sheet of newspaper; the glitter can then be used again.

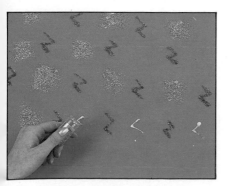

Now use the glue to make more designs and coat these in glitter of a different colour. Localize the sprinkling of the glitter over the new patterns to be covered and leave to dry. Tip off the excess glitter and return it to its container.

Wallpaper is often useful as a gift covering — particularly if your present is very large. Here we have used thick wallpaper with an embossed pattern and given it a touch of style and individuality. Wrap your gift, and choose some wax crayons in contrasting shades. Rub a colour over the raised surface of the wallpaper to highlight one of the motifs in the design.

Choose another colour, and use it to pick out another section in the pattern. (Instead of wax crayons, you could use coloured pencils or chalk; the latter would need to be rubbed with a tissue afterwards to remove loose dust. The medium you choose must slide over the embossing without colouring in the whole design — paint is therefore not suitable.)

Repeat the process using a third colour and continue with as many shades as you like. A tip while wrapping your gift — you'll probably find that ordinary tape will not stick to the surface of wallpaper; double-sided tape used between two folds will be more effective.

All kinds of effects can be achieved with a sponge and some paint. You'll need a piece of natural sponge as man-made sponge doesn't produce the right effect. Choose some plain paper and mix up some poster paint to a fairly runny consistency. Test the paint on a spare piece of paper until you're happy with the colour.

Stencilling is great fun to do — and so easy. Design a simple motif then make a trace of it. With a soft pencil, scribble over the back of the trace and put the tracing paper face up on stencil cardboard. Draw round the design again, pressing hard so that the lines are transferred on to the cardboard beneath. Repeat the motif several times and cut out the shapes with a craft knife.

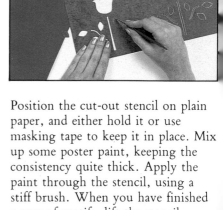

Position the cut-out stencil on plain paper, and either hold it or use masking tape to keep it in place. Mix up some poster paint, keeping the consistency quite thick. Apply the paint through the stencil, using a stiff brush. When you have finished a row of motifs, lift the stencil carefully and blot it on newspaper so that it is ready to use again. Leave the design to dry.

Dab the sponge into the paint and pat it evenly over the paper. The sponge should hold sufficient paint for about four 'dabs' before you need to dip it into the paint again. You'll need to mix up a lot of paint as the sponge absorbs a considerable amount.

Rinse the sponge out well and squeeze dry. When the paper has dried, repeat the process with another colour — you can use as many colours as you wish. Match the ribbon to one of the colours; see page 49 for instructions on how to create the ribbon trim shown here.

Keep repeating the process until you have covered enough paper to wrap your gift. To help you keep the spacing even between each run of motifs, add some 'markers' to the stencil. Cut half a motif at the end of the run and another one above the run to mark the position of the next row. Paint the markers along with the other motifs, then use this image for re-positioning the next row.

Employ a humble potato to create simple yet beautiful designs. Begin by cutting a large potato in half and draw a simple design on it. Use a sharp knife or craft knife to sculp the potato, leaving the design raised from the surface.

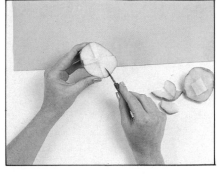

To ensure a regular print, draw a grid lightly in pencil on a sheet of plain paper. Then mix up fairly thick poster paint and apply it to the potato-cut with a paintbrush. Print the design in the middle of each square of the grid. You should be able to do two or three prints before the colour fades and needs replenishing.

Stylish, expensive-looking wrapping paper can be achieved very quickly with this method of spray stencilling. Choose some plain coloured paper for a base, and make your stencils from plain cardboard or paper. Cut the stencils into squares of two different sizes; alternatively you could use any kind of basic shape — stars, circles or whatever.

Cover the whole sheet with one design. Cut another design on another potato half; repeat the whole process, this time printing on the cross of the grid. When the paint is thoroughly dry, rub out the grid lines still visible and wrap up your present.

Lay some of the shapes in a random pattern across the plain paper, holding them in place with a spot of Plasticine or modelling clay. Cover the whole paper with paint spray. Use car paint or craft spray paint, but do carry it out in a well-ventilated room.

Once the paint is dry take off the sprayed squares and put a new random pattern of fresh squares across the paper. Overlap some of the original squares with the new ones to create interesting effects, then spray the entire sheet with a second colour of paint. Remove the squares and leave the wrapping paper to dry before using it.

The delicate silhouette of a doily against a contrasting background colour looks attractive on a gift. Wrap your present up in plain paper and glue the doilies wherever you like. To decorate the corners of a large gift, fold a doily in half, then in half again.

Unfold the doily carefully and spread it out. Cut off one of the quarters of the doily; the folds along which you should cut will be clearly visible.

Paste the doily over one corner of the gift as shown. Repeat with alternate corners, unless your gift has enough space to take a doily over each corner without overlap. The doilies don't have to be white: silver or gold is also effective. Nor do they have to be circular — square ones would be smart on a square-sided present.

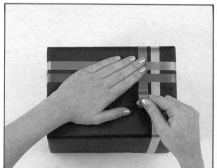

Brightly-coloured adhesive tape can give any plain wrapping paper a touch of style. A geometric design is easiest to create with tape, and the most effective; curves are rather difficult! Work out your design first and measure it out accurately on the parcel in pencil.

Stick the tapes in place along the pencil marks. Take care that the tapes don't stretch at all during application or they will cause the paper to pucker slightly. Sticky tapes are available in an enormous variety of colours, textures and patterns; choose a strong contrast with your paper.

Y̲ou couldn't distinguish this pointed pom-pom from a shop-bought version — yet it's a fraction of the price! Use ribbon which sticks to itself when moistened. Make a small loop by wrapping the ribbon round your thumb; moisten the ribbon and fix it in place. Now twist the ribbon back on itself to form a pointed loop, as shown; stick it in position.

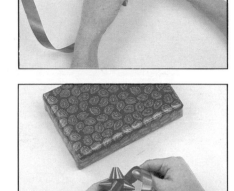

Go on looping the ribbon in twists, spacing them evenly as you go. It is fairly fiddly but keep trying — you'll soon master the technique. You'll probably need to wait a minute between each fixing for the ribbon's glue to dry before turning the next loop.

I̲t's hard to believe that these pretty flowers and the butterfly are made from tights (pantyhose) and fuse wire. Cut up a pair of discarded tights or stockings. Cut some 15 amp fuse wire into lengths, some shorter than others, suitable for making petals. Make a circular shape out of each length and twist the ends together.

Continue winding outwards in a circle until the bow is as big as you want; cut off the ribbon, leaving a small tail just visible. Attach the pom-pom to the present with double-sided tape.

P̲ut a piece of stocking material over a wire circle and pull it tight, making sure that the whole circle is covered. Fix it in position by firmly winding matching cotton around the twisted stem of the wire. Cut off the excess fabric.

Take seven petals, smaller ones in the centre, and bind them all tightly with thread. Bend the petals around until you're happy with the look of the flower. Tie up your parcel with ribbon and attach the flower with double-sided tape. The butterfly is made in just the same way: two pairs of 'petals' are bound together with thread, then bent into the shape of wings.

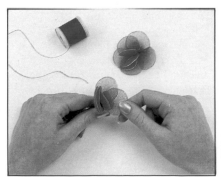

Holly leaves are an attractive shape and perfect for decorating a festive gift. Measure the length of the diagonal across the top of your parcel. On a sheet of plain paper, draw a large holly leaf, the 'vein' of which measures slightly more than half the length of the diagonal.

These Christmas bells ring out gaily from your present. Make two paper templates, both bell-shaped, with one showing the outline of the clapper from the bottom edge. From thin cardboard, cut out two of each shape.

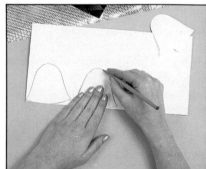

Trace four holly leaves on to some green cardboard, using the template you have just created. Cut the leaves out and bend them in the middle; creasing them slightly where the central vein would be.

Cover all the cardboard shapes with gold paper (or any colour which would co-ordinate with your wrapping paper). Cover both sides, and trim away all the excess paper. On the bell shapes with the clapper, cut a slit from the curved top of the bell to the centre of the bell. On the others (the plain ones) cut a slit from the middle of the bottom edge, also to the centre.

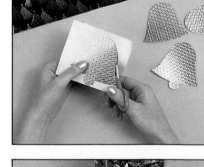

Make the berries from a ball of cotton wool (known as absorbent cotton in the United States) wrapped in two squares of red tissue paper. Put a dab of glue inside and twist up the tissue tightly at the base. When the glue is dry, cut off as much excess of the twist as possible. Group the leaves and berries on the parcel; attach with glue or double-sided tape.

Pierce a hole in the top of the plain bell shapes and thread them with a length of ribbon. Then slot the pairs of bell shapes together (i.e. the plain one, and the one with the clapper) so that they form three-dimensional shapes, as shown here. Tie a group of as many bells as you like on to your gift.

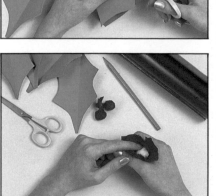

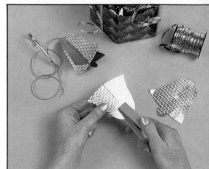

ELIZABETHAN BOW

FLOPPY BOW

The scrolled shapes of this decoration are reminiscent of the curlicues embellishing Queen Elizabeth I's signature. Wrap up your present, and choose some gift wrapping ribbon to match or contrast with the colours of the gift wrap. Hold the end of the ribbon in one hand, and form a loop as shown, leaving a small tail.

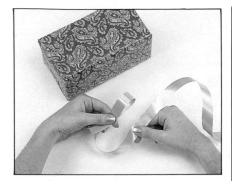

Make a corresponding loop below, forming a figure-of-eight shape. This will be the size of the finished product; adjust the proportion of the loops at this stage if you want a bigger or smaller bow. Continue folding loops of the same size until you have as many as you want — seven at each end is usually enough.

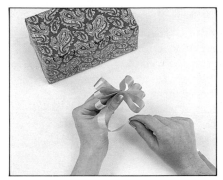

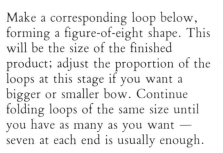

Check that all the loops are the same size, and pinch them all together by wrapping a piece of sticky tape around the middle. You can then hide this by wrapping a small piece of matching ribbon over it. Attach it to the present with double-sided tape.

This bow, with its floppy loops, gives a soft, casual effect. You'll need about 2m (6ft) of acetate or craft ribbon, 2.5cm (1in) wide. Cut off about 30cm (12in) ribbon; wind the rest round your fingers. Holding the ribbon firmly, make a notch in both edges with a pair of scissors as shown, cutting through all the layers of ribbon.

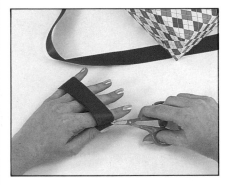

Take the ribbon off your hand and notch the edges of the opposite side of the loops. Flatten the loops so that the notches match in the centre and loops are formed either side. Take the 30cm (12in) length of ribbon and tie it tightly around the notches as shown.

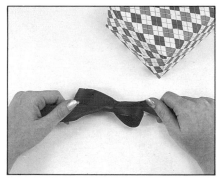

Starting with the innermost loop on one side of the folded bow, gently pull each loop away from the other loops and into the centre of the bow. You'll end up with each loop being visible, thus forming the shape of the finished rosette.

A pom-pom bow adds a cheerful touch to a present of any shape or size. Use the kind of ribbon which will stick to itself when moistened. Cut seven strips; four measuring about 30cm (12in), the other three about 23cm (9in). You'll also need a small piece of ribbon about 5cm (2in), for the central loop.

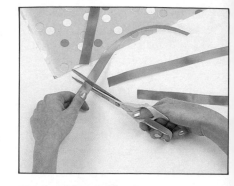

Overlap the ends of each of the long strips and moisten them; stick them together to form a loop. Moisten the centre of each loop and stick it together as shown. Cross two of the looped strips, joining them at the central point. Repeat with the other two loops. Join both crosses together so the loops are evenly spaced apart.

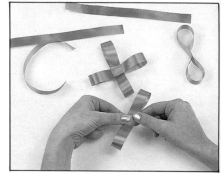

Here is an easy way to achieve a very pretty effect. Choose three colours of narrow ribbon which co-ordinate with your gift wrap. Using one ribbon, tie it around your parcel in the usual way, crossing it underneath the parcel and knotting it tightly on top; leave long ends. Tie a length of different coloured ribbon to the centre point, then do the same with a third colour.

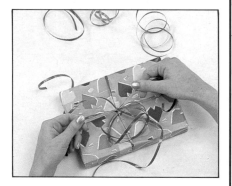

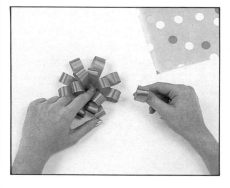

Loop the three shorter lengths, and cross them over each other, fixing them together at the centre. Stick the resulting star in the middle of the large rosette. Fill in the centre with the tiny loop. Obviously, the length and width of ribbon can be varied, according to the size you want the finished pom-pom to be.

Continue tying on lengths of ribbon so that you end up with two lengths, (that is, four ends) of each colour. Tie the central knots tightly to keep them as small as possible. Pull a ribbon length gently along the open blade of a pair of scissors; this will cause it to curl into ringlets. Repeat with each length until they are as curly as you want.

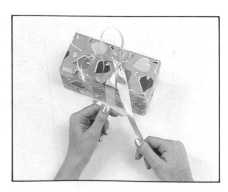

An alternative is to use wide gift ribbon. Tie it round the parcel once, making sure that the knot is as neat as possible and leaving long ends. Cut two small nicks in the ribbon, dividing it evenly into three; pull it to split the ribbon up to the knot. Run each of these lengths along the blade of a pair of scissors until they form ringlets.

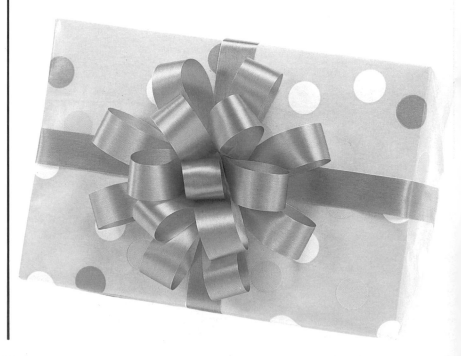

A sweet treat for children of all ages! Boiled sweets (hard candies) with plain cellophane wrappers look best because of their clear colours, but you can use alternatives such as toffees or peppermints. Select five or six of the chosen sweets, and hold them in a bunch by one end of their wrappers.

Take a narrow piece of ribbon and tie all the sweets together tightly; if the wrappers are a little short it may help to bind them first with sewing thread. Leave a reasonably long piece of ribbon on each side of the bunch of sweets so that you can attach it easily to the parcel.

Tie the same ribbon around the parcel, leaving the ends long, then tie the sweets to the centre point as shown. Curl up each ribbon end by pulling it gently along the open blade of a pair of scissors. Try to co-ordinate your gift wrap with the chosen confectionery — black and white paper with humbugs, for example, would look very attractive.

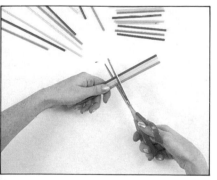

B rightly-coloured drinking straws lend themselves to decorating presents. Look for colours to co-ordinate with your gift wrap. The straws can be made of paper or plastic; both work well. Select the colours you want and cut four straws in half; discard one of each half. Cut another four straws in two, leaving one section slightly longer than the other; retain both pieces.

Place four halves, one of each colour, together over a central point in a star shape and staple them together. Do the same with the other slightly longer straws and their shorter counterparts so that you end up with three stars of slightly different sizes. With the smallest on top and largest on the bottom, staple all three together. Attach the triple star to the parcel with double-sided tape.

Craft foil is the perfect material for creating this decoration. Use a compass to draw four circles; the ones shown here measure 8cm (3in), 6.5cm (2½in) 5cm (2in) and 4cm (1½in) in diameter. Draw an inner ring of 2cm (¾in) in the centre of each circle. Rule lines to divide the circles evenly into eighths; cut along the lines to the inner circle to make eight segments.

Roll each segment of the circle into a cone; use a dab of glue to secure it. Make sure that each cone shape has a good sharp point by rolling it fairly tightly. The process is a bit fiddly; you may find it easier to roll each cone around the point of a stencil to give it shape. Repeat with the other circles.

Starting with the largest star shape, glue all the stars inside each other, positioning the points of each star between those of the preceding ones. When the glue is dry, gently bend each cone of the middle two stars towards the centre, to fill in the central space, so forming a semi-circular three-dimensional star.

A pretty arrangement of dried flowers make a lovely decoration for a gift. You can pick grasses and seedheads in the country or you can dry flowers from your own garden; it's fun and quite easy. Or you can buy them, though of course it's more expensive that way! First cut the dried plants all the same length.

Bunch the flowers together; when you're happy with them, wrap sticky tape around the stalks. Hide the tape by winding ribbon over it. Tie ribbon round the parcel, finish off with a knot, and attach the little bouquet by tying its trailing ribbons over the knot; trim the ends of the bouquet ribbon away. Using the ends of the other ribbon, finish off by making a pretty bow over the bouquet.

ROSEBUDS

A small posy of pretty rosebuds makes a very special decoration for an extra-special gift. Cut a small length of ribbon — about 6-9cm (2-3½in), depending on the width of ribbon you've chosen. Fold the ribbon in half, right sides together, and join the two ends with a small seam. Run a gathering thread around one edge.

Pull the gathering thread tight to form the rosebud; sew it firmly across the base. Make another two or three buds and sew them all together at the base; you may need to add the occasional supporting stitch at the top edges to hold the buds close together.

The leaves add an attractive contrast. They are made from a strip of green ribbon, two corners of which have been folded over to form a point. Fix with double-sided tape since glue can leave a mark on ribbon. The illustration below shows the rosebuds grouped on a length of ribbon twice the width of the flowers, set off with narrow green ribbon.

RIBBON ROSETTES

A winning idea for any gift! Cut a length of fairly wide ribbon; you'll need about 30cm (12in) for each rosette. Fold it in half with the right sides of the ribbon together; sew up the two ends to form a seam.

Using tiny stitches, gather up one edge of the ribbon. Pull the gathering thread tight, arranging the rosette into a neat circle as you do so. Finish it off by sewing across the base. Make as many rosettes as you need and attach them to your parcel with double-sided tape.

These sachets are ideal for ties, soaps, scarves, jewellery, hankies, socks and so forth. On to thin cardboard, trace the template on page 95. It's probably more interesting to cover the shape with gift wrap as shown here, but you can use plain cardboard if you wish. If using gift wrap, cut out the shape and paste it on to your chosen wrapping paper.

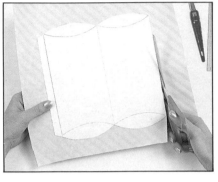

Cut out the covered shape. Then score well along the curved lines of the ellipses which will form the overlapping ends of the packet. Use the back of a craft knife or the blunt side of a pair of scissors to make the score marks.

Stick the side flaps together with either double-sided tape or glue. Fold in the ends; if you've scored the lines sufficiently they should pop in easily with just a little guidance. They can be re-opened with no difficulty, but make sure the covering gift wrap doesn't begin to lift off the cardboard.

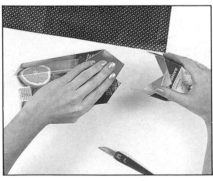

A handy gift container, ideal for home-made sweets, can be made from a well-washed juice carton. Draw V-shapes in each side of the carton. These should be inverted on two opposite sides, and pointing towards the top of the carton on the other two sides. Cut cleanly along the drawn lines with a craft knife as shown.

Cover the carton with gift wrap; adhesive in spray form achieves the best results. Make sure the join lies neatly down one corner of the box. Trim the overlap at the top of the carton so that it is even and fold the paper over the edges, taking care that the corners are neat. Punch a hole at the apex of both the pointed sides and thread ribbon through.

This method is best suited to a small box as the end result is not particularly strong. From thin cardboard, cut out a cross-shaped piece as shown, made up of four sides and a base, all the same size and all absolutely square. The lid will also be a square measuring 5mm (¼in) larger than the base, with sides about 2cm (¾in) deep.

This small narrow box would be ideal for giving someone a watch or a piece of jewellery this Christmas. Trace off the template on page 95 on to thin cardboard. Cut it out, and either cover it in gift wrap or, if you like the colour of the cardboard, just leave it plain.

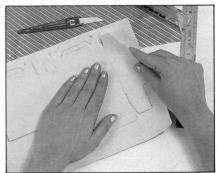

Cut around the template with small sharp scissors to trim away the excess gift wrap; take extra care with the slots and handles. Then score along all the fold lines, using the back of the craft knife or the blunt edge of the scissors.

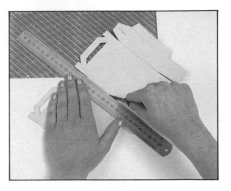

Paste both shapes on to gift wrap and when dry cut off the gift wrap around the box and lid, leaving a small turning or flap around each edge. Fold in the flap on the left of each side of the box and glue it down as shown. Score along the edges of what will be the base, to form fold lines for the sides of the box.

Bend the sides upwards. Put glue on the patterned side of the flaps of gift wrap left unfolded on each side; stick these flaps inside the box to the adjacent sides as illustrated. Crease down the sides firmly and leave to dry. Finally, fold in and glue the top lip. Treat the lid in exactly the same way.

Crease all the folds properly. Fold the box into shape and stick the side flap to the inside of the opposite side. Close the top section, being sure to fold the lid sections upright as shown, halfway across at the point where the two handles meet. Fold over the end flaps and slot them in position to close the box. Finally close the base.

A plant is a notoriously difficult item to wrap; here's a smart solution. Measure an equilateral triangle on some coloured cardboard. The length of each side should be twice the height of the plant; use a protractor to ensure all the angles measure 60°.

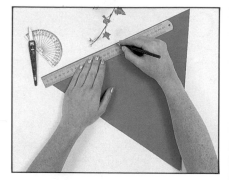

Divide each of the three sides of the triangle in half. Join all the half marks together to form an inner equilateral triangle; this will form the base. Bend the card along a ruler at each inner line as shown and bring up the sides to form a three-dimensional triangle. Punch a hole in each apex and thread ribbon through to close the parcel; double length ribbon gives a pretty finishing touch.

These rigid little boxes are ideal for presenting jewellery but you can make them to fit anything you like. Choose thin cardboard, either in the colour you want the finished box to be, or white so that you can cover it later with gift wrap. Measure out the template on page 95. The size of the triangular sides doesn't matter, as long as they are all the same, and the base is a true square.

Cut out along the exterior lines with a craft knife. If you're covering the cardboard shape with gift wrap, do it at this stage, cutting the paper to fit. Score along all the fold lines carefully, using the back of the craft knife, then bend the box along the score marks, creasing firmly.

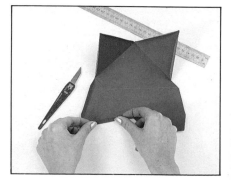

Punch holes in each apex and fold the box into its pyramidal shape. Thread the ribbon in and out of the four holes and, making sure all the side-folds are tucked inside the box, tie the loose ends together with a bow.

Smart handles give this box style; they are also the mechanism for closing it. Use coloured cardboard for the box; if you try to cover the box pattern with gift wrap it will lift off. Copy the template on page 95, scaling it up or down if you wish. Use a compass to draw the handles. Cut out the shape with a craft knife, taking great care with the handles and their slots.

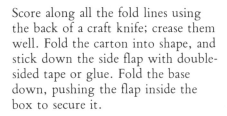

Score along all the fold lines using the back of a craft knife; crease them well. Fold the carton into shape, and stick down the side flap with double-sided tape or glue. Fold the base down, pushing the flap inside the box to secure it.

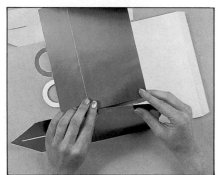

Close the first two flaps of the lid, folding the handles up to fit. Pinch the handles together and fold the two top flaps of the lid over them, fitting the handles through the slots.

Gift bags are very useful as containers for awkwardly-shaped presents and they can be made to any size. Find something with the required dimensions of the finished bag to serve as a mould — a pile of books should suffice. Choose a good quality, strong gift wrap for making the bag. Cut a strip of gift wrap long enough to wrap round the 'mould' and fold over the top edge.

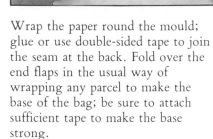

Wrap the paper round the mould; glue or use double-sided tape to join the seam at the back. Fold over the end flaps in the usual way of wrapping any parcel to make the base of the bag; be sure to attach sufficient tape to make the base strong.

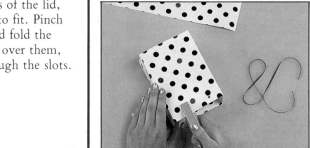

Slip the mould out. Fold in the sides of the bag, creasing them in half at the top; fold the base up over the back of the bag. Punch two holes, spaced apart, at the top of the front and back of the bag as shown. Thread through a length of cord to form a handle; knot each end inside the bag. Repeat on the other side. Alternatively, you could thread the bag with ribbon.

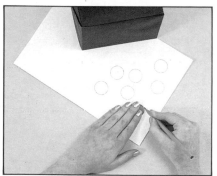

Cube-shaped presents will look more interesting disguised as dice — and it's fun if a small, flat gift becomes a domino. For the dice, make sure the gift is a perfect cube by measuring it; the idea won't work well unless it is. Cover the gift with black paper. Then draw several circles on white paper; an easy way of doing this is by tracing the outline of a suitably sized coin.

Cut out the circles carefully and lay them on the box; glue them in place. Look at a real dice to get the juxtaposition of the sides correct. The domino can be treated in the same way.

Brighten up a dull-looking, flat gift by turning it into a playing card. Wrap the present in plain white paper. Make a template for the spade by folding a piece of paper in half and drawing half the outline against the fold; this way the design will be symmetrical. Trace around the template on to black paper and cut the shape out. Stick the spade in the centre of the 'card'.

Cut two small spades for the corner designs. Then, using a ruler, draw an 'A' in two of the corners, being careful to make them both the same. Glue the small spades underneath. Cut a piece of patterned paper — smaller than the card — and stick it on the back.

Here's a clever idea for disguising a record. Get two large squares of cardboard; the side of a box will do. Position the record in one corner as shown and draw a line from the bottom right corner of the record to the top right corner of the cardboard. Draw a second rule from the top left corner of the record to complete the kite shape. Repeat for the other square.

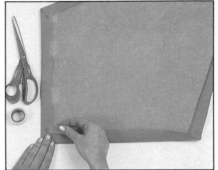

Cut out the shapes and sandwich the record between them. Cover one side in coloured paper, folding over the edges and fixing them with sticky tape on the reverse. Cut another piece of paper slightly smaller than the cardboard shape; glue it in position on the back of the kite.

Draw two lines joining the four corners of the kite, and put contrasting tape along them; take care not to stretch the tape as it will pucker the paper. Cut out as many paper bow shapes as you want for the kite's tail. Attach the bows with double-sided tape or glue to a length of ribbon and stick the tail in position behind the longest point of the kite.

Just the disguise for a cylinder-shaped gift this Xmas — the famous British red pillar-box (mailbox). Cut a strip of thin red cardboard to fit around your gift; secure it around the gift with sticky tape. Draw a circle for the lid, larger than the diameter of the cylinder; cut a line to its centre as shown.

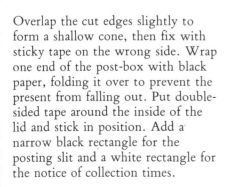

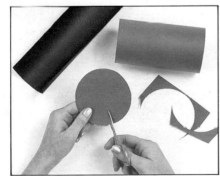

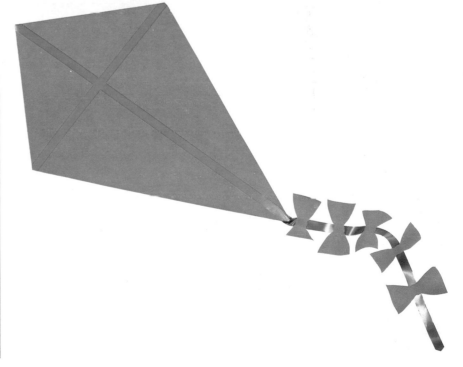

Overlap the cut edges slightly to form a shallow cone, then fix with sticky tape on the wrong side. Wrap one end of the post-box with black paper, folding it over to prevent the present from falling out. Put double-sided tape around the inside of the lid and stick in position. Add a narrow black rectangle for the posting slit and a white rectangle for the notice of collection times.

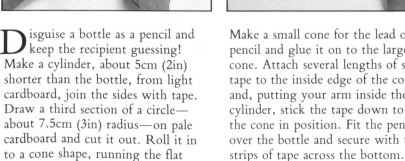

Disguise a bottle as a pencil and keep the recipient guessing! Make a cylinder, about 5cm (2in) shorter than the bottle, from light cardboard, join the sides with tape. Draw a third section of a circle— about 7.5cm (3in) radius—on pale cardboard and cut it out. Roll it in to a cone shape, running the flat edge of a pair of scissors along it to help it curl. Tape in place.

Make a small cone for the lead of the pencil and glue it on to the larger cone. Attach several lengths of sticky tape to the inside edge of the cone and, putting your arm inside the cylinder, stick the tape down to hold the cone in position. Fit the pencil over the bottle and secure with two strips of tape across the bottom.

Bottles of seasonal spirits make an ideal present — but hide such an obvious-looking gift under the decorative guise of a Christmas tree. Find a flower-pot just big enough to take the base of the bottle. From thin cardboard cut out a third section of a large circle and make a deep cone about 8cm (3in) shorter than the bottle. Cover the cone with suitable wrapping paper.

Put the bottle in the flower-pot and place the cone on top. You may need to trim the cone if it seems to cover too much of the flower-pot; do this with care, since you could easily make the cone too short! Double over a piece of tinsel, tie it in a knot and stick it on top of the 'tree'.

Make a small present look that extra bit special — and that extra bit bigger! Wrap the gift into a ball shape, then cut a strip of paper about three times the width of the gift and long enough to form loops on each side of it. Fold the edges over. Gather small pleats at each end, securing them with sticky tape. Pinch-pleat four gathers in the middle of the strip and secure.

What fun for a child to see Frosty and know that the snowman's hiding a gift! Wrap up a cylindrical gift in paper to form the body of the snowman. Crush newspaper into a shape for the head and stick it on top of the gift. Cover the body with cotton wool (absorbent cotton), sticking it on with dabs of glue. Create a face from bits of paper and stick in place.

For the trailing sections of the bow, cut a five-sided piece of paper as shown. Fold over the edges in to the centre at the back and secure with tape. Gather pinch pleats at one end and secure. At the other end cut out a V-shaped section to form a nicely-shaped tail. Repeat the procedure a second time.

For the hat, you need a strip of cardboard, plus a circle big enough to make the brim. Draw an inner circle in the brim, the diameter of Frosty's head; cut it out to form the 'lid' of the hat. Roll the strip of cardboard up to form the crown of the hat; stick it in place with tape.

Turn the pleated ends of the long strip to the middle to form the loops, and secure with double-sided tape. Stick the tails under the bow with more tape. Finally, put double-sided tape over the join on top of the bow and stick the gift in position. Puff out the loops so they look nice and full.

Stick on the top of the hat, then attach the brim, putting strips of tape inside the crown. Paint the hat with black poster paint; it'll need two or three coats. Wrap around the red ribbon to form a cheery hat-band and put it on Frosty's head. Fray the ends of some patterned ribbon to form a scarf and tie it firmly in place.

With so many presents being exchanged at this time of the year, tags are very important. And they are so easy to make. Draw any festive shape you like on to thin cardboard; this one is a Christmas stocking. Cut out the shape and cover it with bright paper; try to co-ordinate the colours with those in the gift wrap you use for your present.

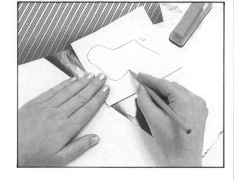

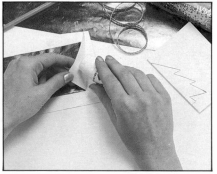

If your wrapping paper has a particular theme in its design make a tag to echo it. To ensure that your design is symmetrical, fold a piece of paper in half and draw on half the design against the fold. Cut around the outline through both layers of paper; open out and use this as a template for the design. Cover a piece of light cardboard with gift wrap and trace around the template.

Cut around the outline and punch a hole at the top of the tag. Write your message and tie the tag on to the parcel. You could cheat a little when designing the shape of your tag by tracing an illustration from a magazine or by using the outline of a pastry cutter.

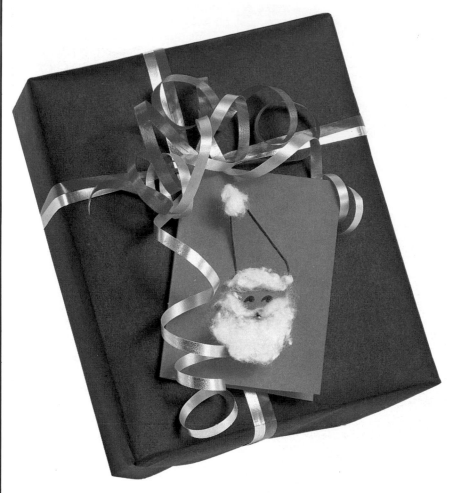

A three-dimensional Santa Claus tag, complete with fluffy beard, provides a jolly festive decoration on a gift. Draw a fairly large rectangle on thin red cardboard; make sure that all the corners are right angles. Score down the middle and fold the cardboard, creasing it well. Draw an inverted 'V' for Santa's hat, and a curve for his chin; cut them out with a craft knife.

Curve the hat and chin outward to give them a three-dimensional look, then draw in the eyes and mouth. Form a beard from a small piece of cotton wool (absorbent cotton), and stick it in position with a dab of glue. Do the same with the fur trim on the edge of the hat and the pom-pom on its tip. Punch a hole in the back of the label, write your message and tie the tag on the parcel.

Aheavenly messenger bears the greetings on this Christmas present. Cut a quarter section of a circle from light cardboard to form a narrow cone for the body. On a folded piece of paper draw one arm and one wing against the edge of the fold as shown, so that when they are cut out you will have a pair of each.

Used greeting cards can often be turned into very acceptable gift tags. Sometimes, as here, the design lends itself to forming a tag. Cut very carefully around the lines of the motif you want to use. Make a hole with a punch, thread a ribbon through the hole and no one would guess the tag had a previous life!

Make the cone and cover it with silver paper (aluminium foil would do). Trace the arm and wings on to silver paper; cut them out and glue them in their relevant positions on the body.

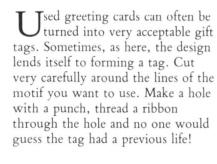

Sometimes a little imagination is needed to give the tag a new and ready-made look. Here, the shape of the tag is outlined on the cardboard in red with a felt-tipped pen. Draw the outline lightly in pencil first to be absolutely sure it is the right size and shape to create the finished label.

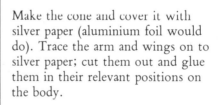

Make the head by rolling up some white tissue paper into a firm ball, twisting the ends of the tissue tightly to form a 'neck'. Glue the head into the top of the cone. Tie a scrap of tinsel into a loose knot and stick it on the head as a halo. Make a scroll from white paper, write on your message and stick it between the angel's hands. Attach the angel to the gift with double-side tape.

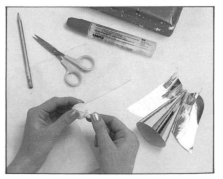

There can be no doubt who these presents are for! It's fun to make a tag out of the initial or — even better — the whole name of the recipient. First draw the shape of the letters you want on to a piece of tracing paper. Make sure that the letters in a name interlock sufficiently.

When you're happy with the result, trace the letters (or single initial) on to coloured cardboard, pressing hard to make a clear outline. Use a ruler where there are straight sections to a letter.

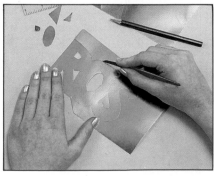

Create a stylish effect by matching the tag to the ribbon. Plain ribbon with a strongly patterned paper is attractive but a tartan ribbon with plain paper can look stunning. And if you don't have any ribbon, even a strip of fabric cut out with pinking shears will suffice! Glue a length of ribbon or fabric on to thin cardboard to make it rigid.

Trim away any excess cardboard. Fold the stiffened ribbon over and cut it to the length you want the finished tag to be. Punch a hole through your newly-created tag and thread a piece of contrasting narrow ribbon through the hole to tie it to the parcel. Trim the edges of the tag to match the ends of the bow.

Next, cut out the shape using a craft knife, carefully following the traced lines. Punch a hole in a position where the weight of the tag will make it hang well on the gift.

Smart Sachets (page 84)

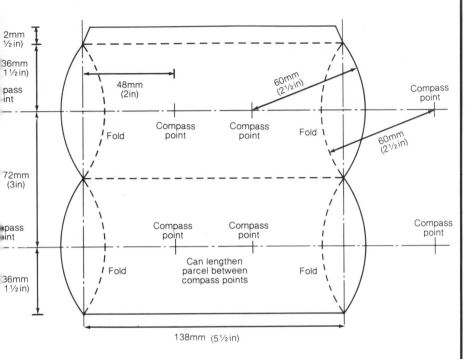

2mm (½ in)

36mm (1½ in)

pass int

48mm (2in)

60mm (2½ in)

Compass point

Fold

Compass point

Compass point

Fold

Compass point

60mm (2½ in)

72mm (3in)

pass int

Compass point

Compass point

Compass point

Fold

Can lengthen parcel between compass points

Fold

36mm (1½ in)

138mm (5½ in)

Boxed In (page 85)

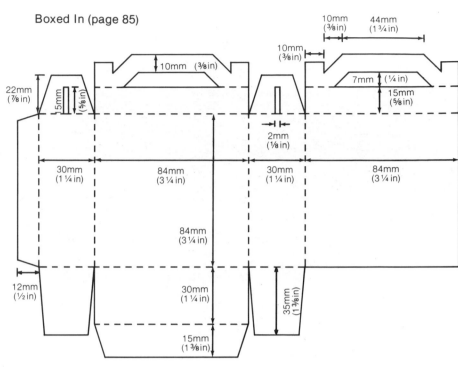

10mm (⅜ in)

44mm (1¾ in)

10mm (⅜ in)

22mm (⅞ in)

10mm (⅜ in)

7mm (¼ in)

15mm (⅝ in)

15mm (⅝ in)

2mm (⅛ in)

30mm (1¼ in)

84mm (3¼ in)

30mm (1¼ in)

84mm (3¼ in)

84mm (3¼ in)

12mm (½ in)

30mm (1¼ in)

35mm (1⅜ in)

15mm (1⅜ in)

The Pyramids (page 86)

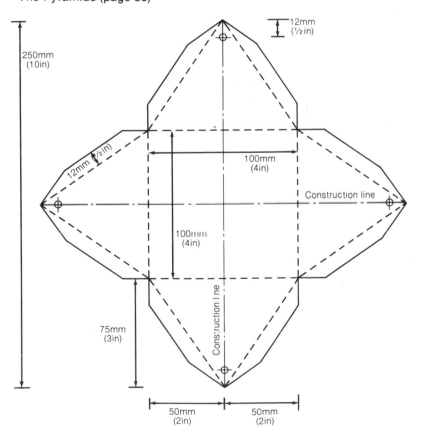

12mm (½ in)

250mm (10in)

12mm (½ in)

100mm (4in)

Construction line

100mm (4in)

Construction line

75mm (3in)

50mm (2in)

50mm (2in)

Handle With Care! (page 87)

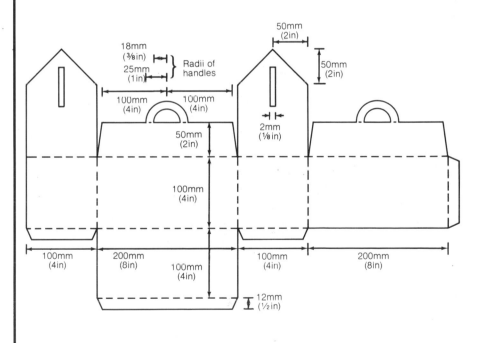

18mm (⅜ in)

25mm (1in)

Radii of handles

50mm (2in)

50mm (2in)

100mm (4in)

100mm (4in)

50mm (2in)

2mm (⅛ in)

100mm (4in)

100mm (4in)

200mm (8in)

100mm (4in)

200mm (8in)

100mm (4in)

12mm (½ in)

SCIENTIFIC CLASSIFICATION

The following is an alphabetical list of the common names of plants
used in this book and their Latin equivalents

Common name	Latin name	Common name	Latin name
Baby's breath	*Gypsophilia paniculata*	Oak	*Quercus*
Bottlebrush	*Callistemon*	Pearl everlasting	*Anaphalis*
Carnation	*Dianthus*	Poppy	*Papaver*
Chinese lantern	*Physalis*	Rhodanthe (sunray)	*Rhodanthe manglesii =*
Clubrush	*Scirpus*		*Helipterum manglesii*
Cypress	*Cupressus*	Rabbit's or hare's	*Lagarus ovatus*
Glixia (grass daisy)	*Aphyllanthes*	tail grass	
	monspeliensis	Rose	*Rosa*
Holly	*Ilex aquifolium*	Safflower	*Carthamus tinctorius*
Honesty	*Lunaria annua*	Sandflower	*Ammobium alatum*
(silver dollar plant)		Sea lavender	*Limonium tataricum*
Ivy	*Hedera*	September flower	*Aster ericoides*
Larkspur	*Delphinium consolida*	Spruce	*Picea*
Lavender	*Lavandula angustifolia*	Statice	*Limonium sinuatum*
Lily	*Lilium*	Strawflower	*Helichrysum*
Love-lies-bleeding	*Amaranthus caudatus*	(or everlasting)	
Nippleworth (Dutch	*Laspana communis*	Sunray	*Helipterum*
exporters call it broom bloom)		Yarrow	*Achillea*

INDEX

A
A la Carton **84**
Amaranthus **57**
Ammobium **61**
Anaphalis **57**
Angel's Message **93**
A Point to Remember **77**
Autumn Gold **36**
Awkward Angles **72**

B
Baby's breath **64**
Bags of Goodies **87**
Baubles **13, 23**
Bells **9, 14, 20, 21, 78**
Bottlebrush **66, 67**
Bow-shaped gift wrap **91**
Boxed In **85**
Boxes, gift **50, 84-87**
Broom bloom **57, 69**
Butterfly, The **43**
Buttons and Bows **91**
By Candlelight **63**

C
Candle Centrepiece **59**
Candle designs **39, 58, 59, 60, 61**
Candy Crackers **29**
Carnation **64, 65**
Celophane wrapping paper **72**
Centrepieces **35-39, 57-61**
Champagne and Roses **65**

Charlie Clown **31**
Chinese lantern **62, 68**
Christmas Candles **61**
Christmas Card Garland **28**
Christmas card tags **93**
Christmas Cheer **90**
Christmas Leaves **78**
Christmas Splendour **62**
Christmas Star **15**
Christmas stocking **12, 47**
Christmas trees **6, 7, 8, 16**
Christmas Tree Cake **35**
Christmas tree decorations **9-15, 68, 69**
Christmas tree designs **11, 19, 35, 40, 47, 90, 92**
Christmas Tree Novelties **69**
Christmas Tree Treats **12**
Christmas Trellis **28**
Chrysanthemum **64**
Cinnamon **68**
Clowning Around **30**
Clown mask **31**
Clubrush **67**
Colouring Book **73**
Cone Candle Stand **39**
Cones **16, 36, 54, 55, 57, 59, 60, 61, 66, 68**
Crackers **13, 29, 37, 48, 49**
Crepe Paper Chain **25**
Cressia **66, 67**
Crown **31**
Crowning Glory **31**
Cypress **58**

D
Delicate Doilies **76**
Design with a Sponge **74**
Dice gift wrap **88**
Ding Dong Merrily **78**
Doilies, paper **7, 76**
Double Cornet **45**
Double Jabot **42**
Drawing Straws **81**
Drinks Party **63**

E
Edible decorations **12, 24, 29**
Eight-Pointed Star **22**
Elizabethan Bow **79**
Ever-Increasing Circles **26**
Everlasting **53, 55, 59, 61, 62, 63, 66, 68, 69**
Everlasting Wreath **18**
Expanding Chain **27**

F
Fairy on the Tree **15**
Fancy Foil **23**
Felt Christmas Tree **19**
Fern **59, 65**
Festive Fern **65**
Festive Floral Plane **66**
Festive Framing **67**
Festive Miniatures **68**
Fleur-de-Lys Fold **45**
Fleur-de-Lys Tablecloth **40**
Flimsy Flowers **26**

Floppy Bow **79**
Floral Decoration **82**
Floral designs **52-69, 82**
Floral Peardrop **53**
Forest Foliage **60**
Freesia **60**
Frosted Fruit **37**
Frosty the Snowman **91**
Fruit centrepieces **36, 37**

G
Get It Taped **76**
Gift boxes **50, 84-87**
  hanging Christmas tree **10**
Gift Box Pom-Pom **50**
Gifts for the table **50, 51**
Gift tags **92-94**
Gift-Wrapped Soaps **51**
Gift wrapping **70-95**
Glamorous Gift Bag **51**
Glitter Glamour **73**
Glitter Tree Placemat **40**
Glitzy Fruit Bowl **36**
Glixia **69**
Go For Gold **6**
Gold and Silver Crackers **37**
Golden Touch **41**
Golden Wreath **55**
Graceful Bells **20**
Grass daisy **29**
Gypsophilia **7, 64**

H
Handle with Care! **87**
Hand-Painted Fruit Basket **38**
Hanging Boxes **10**
Hanging Lanterns **14**
Hare's tail grass **57**
Harlequin Masks **32**
Heather **55**
Helichrysum **53, 55, 59, 61, 62, 63, 66, 68, 69**
Holiday Centrepiece **39**
Holly **41, 58, 59, 64, 65**
Holly leaf design **78**
Honesty **62, 63**
Hoop-La! **21**
Hydrangea **63**

I J K
In Full Bloom **52**
Ivy **36, 41, 59, 60**
Ivy-Candle Ring **60**
Jolly Santa **92**
Jonquil **65**
Kite gift wrap **89**
Kite Place Card **46**

L
Lantern, Christmas tree **14**
Larkspur **53, 57**
Lavender **53, 69**
Lavender Fair **53**
Let's Go Fly a Kite **89**
Let's Pretend **13**
Leucodendron brunia **53, 66, 69**
Leucodendron plumosum **66**
Lily **64**
Little Boxes **85**
Little Crackers **13**
Long-eared pods **62**
Love-lies-bleeding **57**
Lovely Lace **7**
Lucky Dice **88**

M
Mallalika **64**
Marzipan Fruit Parcels **38**
Masks **31, 32**
Masque Ball **32**
Miniature Christmas Tree **16**
Mini Trees **11**
Moss **53, 54, 56, 58, 66**

N O
Name Dropping **94**
Napkin folds **42-45**
Napkin ring **41**
Nipplewort **57, 69**
Oak leaves **61**
Oriental Fan **44**

P Q
Paper chains **25, 26, 27**
Party hats **30, 31**
Pastry Place Marker **47**
Pearl everlasting **57**
Pencil gift wrap **90**
Picture Frame Foliage **16**
Pierrot Hat **30**
Pillar-box gift wrap **89**
Ping Pong Puddings **9**
Pittosporum **64**
Placemat **40**
Playing card gift wrap **88**
Play Your Cards Right **88**
Poinsettia **64**
Pointed Star **82**
Pom-poms, ribbon **77**
Poppy heads **61**
Potato-cut wrapping paper **75**
Potato Prints **75**
Pot-pourri **53**
Presents by Post **89**
Pretty Pastels **8**
Princess, The **43**
Proteus **66**
Pure and Simple **44**
Pure Elegance **42**
Pyramids, The **86**
Quaking grass **53, 68**

R
Rabbit's tail grass **57**
Red Hot Crackers **49**
Resplendence **56**
Rhodanthe **54**
Ribbon Pom-Poms **80**
Ribbon Ringlets **80**
Ribbon Rosettes **83**
Ribbon Tree **17**
Ring-a-Ding **14**
Rose **53, 57, 61, 65, 83**
Rosebuds **83**
Ruscus **61**
Russet Glory **66**
Rustic Centrepiece **61**

S
Safflower **59**
Sandflower **61**
Santa Faces **11**
Satin Presents **10**
Scalloped Squares **27**
Scottish Salute **57**
Sea lavender **54, 55, 59**
Season's Greetings **92**
September flower **64, 65**
Shiny Foil Chain **25**
Silver Bells **21**

Silver dollar plant **62**
Smart Sachets **84**
Snowflake **22**
Snowman gift wrap **91**
South African daisy **63, 68**
Spirited Away **90**
Sponged wrapping paper **74**
Spray and Paint Paper **75**
Spruce **59**
Square Gift Box **50**
Stars **15, 22, 23**
Statice **54**
Stencilled Wrapping Paper **74**
Stirlingia **53**
Stocking Fillers **12**
Stockings, Christmas **12, 47**
Strawflower **53, 55, 59, 61, 62, 63, 66, 68, 69**
Straws, drinking **81**
Sugar Bells **9**
Sunray **54, 59, 63, 66**
Sweet Scent **69**
Sweets for My Sweet **81**
Sweets Galore **24**
Sweet Tooth Tree **8**

T
Table cloth design **40**
Table decorations **34-51, 58-61**
Tartan designs **7, 46, 57, 67, 94**
Tartan Place Card **46**
Tartan Tag **94**
Tartan Ties **7**
Tassel Napkin Ring **41**
Teddy Place Marker **47**
Templates **33, 95**
Tinsel Bells **20**
Top Hat **64**
Traditional Crackers **48**
Triangular Treats **86**
Twinkle Twinkle **23**

U V W
Victorian Cracker **49**
Wallpaper gift wrap **73**
Walnuts **61, 68**
Warm Welcome **59**
Waste Not, Want Not **93**
Winter Solstice **68**
Winter's Tale, A **54**
Wired for Fun **77**
Wiring dried flowers **52**
Wrapping a Cylinder **71**
Wrapping a Rectangle **71**
Wrapping a Sphere **72**
Wrapping paper **73-75**
Wreaths **18, 21, 54, 55, 56, 57, 58, 59**

X Y Z
Yarrow **54, 55, 59**
Yuletide Garland **29**